Resolving Aristotle's Aporia on Time

Jan H. Nylund

Resolving Aristotle's Aporia on Time

palgrave
macmillan

Jan H. Nylund
Centre for Theology and Religious Studies
Lund University
Lund, Sweden

ISBN 978-3-031-65009-3   ISBN 978-3-031-65010-9   (eBook)
https://doi.org/10.1007/978-3-031-65010-9

© The Editor(s) (if applicable) and The Author(s), under exclusive license to Springer Nature Switzerland AG 2024
This work is subject to copyright. All rights are solely and exclusively licensed by the Publisher, whether the whole or part of the material is concerned, specifically the rights of translation, reprinting, reuse of illustrations, recitation, broadcasting, reproduction on microfilms or in any other physical way, and transmission or information storage and retrieval, electronic adaptation, computer software, or by similar or dissimilar methodology now known or hereafter developed.
The use of general descriptive names, registered names, trademarks, service marks, etc. in this publication does not imply, even in the absence of a specific statement, that such names are exempt from the relevant protective laws and regulations and therefore free for general use.
The publisher, the authors and the editors are safe to assume that the advice and information in this book are believed to be true and accurate at the date of publication. Neither the publisher nor the authors or the editors give a warranty, expressed or implied, with respect to the material contained herein or for any errors or omissions that may have been made. The publisher remains neutral with regard to jurisdictional claims in published maps and institutional affiliations.

This Palgrave Macmillan imprint is published by the registered company Springer Nature Switzerland AG.
The registered company address is: Gewerbestrasse 11, 6330 Cham, Switzerland

Paper in this product is recyclable.

To my wife Maria for her passionate and unceasing support

Preface

The question of how to understand the set of *aporiai* in *Physics* IV.10 arose after having studied Aristotle's account of time in *Physics* IV.10-14 over a longer period during research stays at Tyndale House (affiliated to the University of Cambridge) in 2016–17, 2018. I slowly realised that there were a number of outstanding issues that must be dealt with before the text as a whole can be understood. Among these issues were Aristotle's concept of time relative to Plato's account of time in the *Timaeus*, the difficult relative clause ὅ ποτε ὄν that frequently occurs in key passages in Aristotle's account of time and, finally, the *aporiai* in *Physics* IV.10. It was striking to note that on the one hand some interpreters would accept the *aporiai* as literal research questions that seamlessly connect to Aristotle's following so-called positive account of time, whereas others would treat them mostly as nonsense to be rejected. This disparity of opinion called for a thorough enquiry into the nature and claims of the *aporiai*.

I started to work on this issue during a research stay in 2017 at the Department of Ancient Studies at Stellenbosch University (South Africa), but then put it aside due to more pressing matters. A few years later I had opportunities to work with this issue again during research stays at Université Paris 1 Panthéon Sorbonne (2019), Munich School of Ancient Philosophy (2021), the Department of Philosophy at Oslo University (2022) and back home in Lund.

In my opinion a successful exegetical analysis of the *aporiai* depends on (i) a careful reading and analysis (and translation) of the Greek text, (ii) a full reading and analysis of the entire book of *Physics*, (iii) knowledge of Plato's account of time in the *Timaeus*, (iv) knowledge of Aristotle's metaphysics/*Metaphysics*, (v) a proper understanding of what an *aporia* may consist in (in view of the occurrence of different types), and specifically the ones in *Physics* IV.10, and (vi) an understanding of the cognitive-perceptual language of Aristotle vis-à-vis modern cognitive science and cognitive linguistics which I take to be anticipated by Aristotle.

It is with this set of resources that I approach the *aporiai* in an attempt to present a persuasive argument towards an *euporia*, a solution.

Lund, Sweden   Jan H. Nylund

Acknowledgements

I would in particular like to thank David Westberg (Uppsala University) and Thomas Kjeller Johansen (Oslo University) for offering me feedback and suggesting changes and additions towards improving my text. I would also like to thank the anonymous reviewer from Palgrave Macmillan for suggestions towards improvements. Thanks also go to Francesco Fronterotta (La Sapienza, Università di Roma) for his advice regarding how to translate an Italian term. I am also grateful to Johan Thom (Stellenbosch University) for introducing me to classical studies and giving me feedback on my first texts on Aristotle's concept of time.

I would also like to thank the following foundations that to some or a considerable extent have supported my work financially: Axel and Margaret Ax:son Johnson Foundation, Helge Ax:son Johnsons Stiftelse, Knut and Alice Wallenberg Foundation, Magnus Pfannestills Stiftelse, Olaus Petristiftelsen, Stiftelsen landshövding Per Westlings minnesfond, Stiftelsen Olle Engkvist Byggmästare, Svensk-Franska Stiftelsen and The Birgit Rausing Language Programme.

Contents

1 Introduction — 1

2 Previous Research — 5

3 The Concept of ἀπορία — 13

4 The ἀπορίαι in Physics 217b33–218a30 — 23
   4.1 Introduction — 24
   4.2 Ἀπορία 1: Physics 217b33–218a3 — 25
   4.3 Ἀπορία 2: Physics 218a3–8 — 28
   4.4 Ἀπορία 3: Physics 218a8–30 — 29

5 Identifying the Aporetic Contrasts — 35
   5.1 Introduction — 36
   5.2 The Existence or Non-existence of Time — 38
   5.3 Time as Infinite Past and Future or Eternal 'Now' — 40
   5.4 Time as a Cognitive-Perceptive or Logical Category — 40
   5.5 Time as Partaker of Substance or Not — 41
   5.6 'Nows' as the Parts of Time or Not — 42
   5.7 The 'Now' as Different or Same — 43

6	**Resolving the Aporetic Contrasts in Context**	45
	6.1 *Introduction*	47
	6.2 *In Context: The Existence or Non-existence of Time*	48
	6.3 *In Context: Time as Infinite Past and Future or Eternal 'Now'*	55
	6.4 *In Context: Time as a Cognitive-Perceptive or a Mathematical-Logical Category*	57
	6.5 *In Context: Time as Partaker of Substance or Not*	62
	6.6 *In Context: 'Nows' as the Parts of Time or Not*	68
	6.7 *In Context: The 'Now' as Different or Same*	71
7	**Conclusion: From Aporia (ἀπορία) to Euporia (εὐπορία)**	77
	Bibliography	81
	General Index	87
	Index Locorum	93

About the Author

Jan Nylund (Lund University) has over the last years done research within ancient philosophy, particularly on Aristotelian metaphysics, Plato's and Aristotle's concept of time and Stoic thinking on time. During this period he has been a visiting researcher at Tyndale House (affiliated to the University of Cambridge), Stellenbosch University, The Swedish Institute in Rome, Copenhagen University (Centre for the Aristotelian Tradition), Université Paris 1 Panthéon Sorbonne (Le centre GRAMATA), La Sapienza Università di Roma, Munich School of Ancient Philosophy and Oslo University.

He is also a New Testament scholar and has done research and published within Greek linguistics and particularly on the potential of general linguistics in the study of Ancient Greek, such as his recent volume, *The Potential of Linguistic Theories in the Study of Aspect and Tense in Ancient Greek, With Particular Attention to New Testament Greek* (2024).

CHAPTER 1

Introduction

Abstract *Physics* IV.10 contains Aristotle's triple *aporia* on time and what often is referred to as Aristotle's negative account of time, in contrast with his so-called positive account in *Physics* IV.11–14. As opposed to in other cases when Aristotle puts forth *aporias*, no solution to his triple *aporia* on time is offered at the end of his account. The triple *aporia* is perplexing in nature and serves to bring the enquirer to a zero point where he must admit to not really knowing anything certain about time; this humbling experience wipes the slate clean, making room for new fresh thoughts. 'Aporia' may either refer to a state of mind of perplexity, caused by the object of study, or to the problem itself as it is stated in terms of an aporetic contrast. Few, if any, studies have dealt with the *aporia* in *Physics* IV.10 by a full enquiry into the entire context of *Physics* IV.11–14 as well as the entire book of *Physics*. A successful enquiry depends on (1) a careful reading and analysis of the Greek text, (2) a careful study of the entire book of *Physics*, (3) knowledge of Plato's account of time in the *Timaeus*, (4) knowledge of Aristotle's metaphysics/*Metaphysics*, (5) an understanding of what constitutes an *aporia* and particularly the ones in *Physics* IV.10, and (6) an understanding of Aristotle's cognitive-perceptual language as he anticipates thoughts in modern cognitive science. On this basis the triple *aporia* can be dealt with towards reaching an *euporia*, a solution.

© The Author(s), under exclusive license to Springer Nature Switzerland AG 2024
J. H. Nylund, *Resolving Aristotle's Aporia on Time*,
https://doi.org/10.1007/978-3-031-65010-9_1

Keywords Aporia • Aporetic contrast • *Physics* IV.10 • Negative account of time • Positive account of time • Plato • *Timaeus* • *Metaphysics* • Perplexity • *Aporia* as state of mind • *Aporia* as object of study • *Euporia* • Cognition • Cognitive science

At the beginning of *Physics* IV.10, we find a triple ἀπορία on issues related to Aristotle's following discussion on the concept of time. The question is how to understand these ἀπορίαι and what their function is. Aristotle often starts out a discussion on any given topic by putting forth conflicting viewpoints, usually followed up by a solution at the end of the discussion—but not so in his investigation of the concept of time in *Physics* IV.10–14.[1] This is one of the reasons why the function of the ἀπορίαι in *Physics* IV.10 is a matter of debate. Another reason is the apparent contradictions between the elements of the ἀπορίαι, on the one hand, and the contrast that the ἀπορίαι present relative to the rest of Aristotle's chapters on time, on the other. Hence the established reference to the ἀπορίαι as Aristotle's *negative account* of time as opposed to his *positive account* of time in chapters 11–14.

In this study I argue that the ἀπορίαι in *Physics* IV.10 were not constructed to be understood as a presentation of factual issues harmonising with the following chapters of Aristotle's positive account of time. Instead, they are rather aporetic, i.e. 'perplexing,' statements, purposed, on the one hand, to bring the reader to some kind of zero point of acknowledging that one does not really know anything certain about the nature of time[2]—this is ἀπορία in the mental, subjective sense of the word—and, on the other, to function as a dialectically structured textual tool by which the aporetic contrasts are assessed towards gaining new knowledge—this is ἀπορία in the objective, textual sense of the word.

---

[1] Edward Grant, *A History of Natural Philosophy: From the Ancient World to the Nineteenth Century* (Cambridge: Cambridge University Press, 2007), 46; Karl-Heinz Ilting, "Aporie," in *Handbuch philosophischer Grundbegriffe*, (München: Kösel-Verlag, 1973), 113.

[2] After her brief account of the main points of the ἀπορίαι, Andrea Falcon spontaneously captures their effect, "It should not be overlooked that it [running through the puzzles] has also left us with an initial, though confused, grasp of the nature of time (Andrea Falcon, "Aristotle on Time and Change," ed. Hether Dyke and Adrian Bardon, (Oxford: Wiley Blackwell, 2013), 50).

My claim that the ἀπορίαι are aporetic (obviously!) is in itself neither novel nor provocative, but the fact is that few contributors to the discussion have treated them as precisely that and few have been able to offer a creative and well-founded argument to that effect. The ἀπορίαι are not interpretive keys and governing statements, serving as a point of departure for the following analysis in *Physics* IV.11–14 and harmonising, as they stand, with Aristotle's positive account of time in the following chapters.

In terms of focused, in-depth studies of the ἀπορίαι in *Physics* IV:10 from the viewpoint of *Physics* IV.11–14 and the *Physics* as a whole, hardly any attempts have been made. There is thus an acute need for a thorough and rigorous study of these important ἀπορίαι that introduce the first attempt in the history of philosophy to formulate a full and coherent theory on time. The understanding of the status of the ἀπορίαι and the validity of the claims contained in them is to a considerable extent decisive for how Aristotle's following chapters on time are interpreted.

My contention is that a successful exegetical analysis of the ἀπορίαι depends on (i) a careful reading and analysis (and translation) of the Greek text, (ii) a full reading and analysis of the entire book of *Physics*, (iii) knowledge of Plato's account of time in the *Timaeus*, (iv) knowledge of Aristotle's metaphysics/*Metaphysics*, (v) a proper understanding of what an ἀπορία may consist in (in view of the occurrence of different types), and specifically the ones in *Physics* IV.10, and (vi) an understanding of the cognitive-perceptual language of Aristotle vis-à-vis modern cognitive science and cognitive linguistics, which I take to be anticipated by Aristotle.

In Chap. 2, I account for previous research, and then (Chap. 3) account for the concept of ἀπορία among ancient interpreters. After noting (Sect. 4.1) the placement of the aporetic material within a negative *inclusio* and closely analysing (Sects. 4.2–4.4) what Aristotle is actually saying in his three ἀπορίαι,[3] I discuss (Sect. 5.1) how the concept of ἀπορία may be applied to our aporetic text and demonstrate (Sects. 5.2–5.7) that the set of ἀπορίαι is replete with internally irreconcilable contrasts, whether explicitly or implicitly so. The question that naturally arises at this point is whether the ἀπορίαι are just nonsense or whether there are elements that would hold up in a closer analysis. After rehearsing (Sect. 6.1) what the

---

[3] All translations of Greek texts into English are my own except when otherwise indicated.

resolving of an ἀπορία/aporetic contrast entails, I deal (Sects. 6.2–6.7) with this issue by placing the aporetic contrasts in Sects. 5.2–5.7 in the broader context of *Physics* IV.11–14 as well as the *Physics* as a whole, in an attempt to work out which claims hold water and which ones must be rejected or, alternatively, be reformulated: this is the road from ἀπορία towards εὐπορία, a resolving of the aporetic challenge. In Chap. 7 I briefly offer my conclusions.

CHAPTER 2

Previous Research

Abstract Though it is universally recognised among contributors to the discussion that the *aporiai* are precisely that, few treat them as perplexing, humbling statements intended to wipe the slate clean to open up for new fresh thoughts in the direction of gaining new knowledge. Previous contributions can roughly be positioned on a scale ranging from those who fully accept the *aporiai* as they stand, aiming to resolve them on that premise, to those who reject them entirely, treating them as pure nonsense, satisfied to move on to the analysis of Aristotle's following positive account of time. Such a disparity of opinion begs the question as to what the nature of an *aporia* is and in particular the ones in *Physics* IV.10.

Keywords Simplicius • Themistius • Philoponus • Hervé Barreau • Norman Kretzmann • Richard Sorabji • David Bolotin • Elena Cavagnaro-Stuijt • Walter Mesch • Jon McGinnis • Ursula Coope • Jorge Torres • Tony Roark • Andra Striowski • Nathanael Stein • Thomas Seissl • Michael Bruder • Pierre-Luc Boudreault • Michael Inwood • Andra Striowski • Chelsea Harry

© The Author(s), under exclusive license to Springer Nature
Switzerland AG 2024
J. H. Nylund, *Resolving Aristotle's Aporia on Time*,
https://doi.org/10.1007/978-3-031-65010-9_2

Among the contributions[1] to the study of the ἀπορίαι in *Physics* IV.10, we find articles by Norman Kretzmann,[2] David Bolotin,[3] Jon McGinnis,[4] Jorge Torres[5] and Nathanael Stein,[6] book chapters by Richard Sorabji[7] and Michael Inwood,[8] three monographs on Aristotle's concept of time in *Physics* IV.10–14 by Elena Cavagnaro-Stuijt,[9] Ursula Coope[10] and Tony Roark,[11] two dissertations by Michael Bruder and Pierre-Luc Boudreault on Aristotle's time concept,[12] two volumes on related topics by Andra Striowski[13] and Chelsea Harry,[14] one volume by Walter Mesch on time and

---

[1] I do not claim this to be a complete list of contributions to the study of the ἀπορίαι in *Physics* IV.10.

[2] Norman Kretzmann, "Time Exists-but Hardly, or Obscurely," *Proceedings of the Aristotelian Society, Supplementary Volumes (Published by Wiley-Blackwell on behalf of the Aristotelian Society)*, 50, (1976): 91–114.

[3] David Bolotin, "Aristotle's Discussion of Time: An Overview," *Ancient Philosophy* 17, (1997): 47–62.

[4] Jon McGinnis, "Making Time Aristotle's Way," *Apeiron* 36, no. 2 (2003): 143–170; Jon McGinnis, "A Review of Tony Roark: Aristotle on Time: A Study of Physics," *Philosophical Review* XXXII, no. 6 (2012): 518–520.

[5] Jorge Torres, "La aporética del tiempo: Un análisis reconstructivo de Fis. Δ 10, 217b29–218b20," *Ordia Prima* 8/9, (2009/2010): 211–234; I would like to thank Stephen H. Levinsohn for improving on my translations from Spanish into English.

[6] Nathanael Stein, "Aristotle on Parts of Time and Being in Time," *The Review of Metaphysics* 69, no. 3 (2016): 495–518.

[7] Richard Sorabji, *Time, Creation and the Continuum: Theories in Antiquity and the Early Middle Ages* (London: Duckworth, 1983).

[8] Michael Inwood, "Aristotle on the Reality of Time," in *Aristotle's Physics: A Collection of Essays*, ed. Lindsay Judson, (Oxford: Oxford University Press, 1991).

[9] Elena Cavagnaro-Stuijt, *Aristotele e il tempo: analisi di Physica, 4.10–14* (Bologna: Il mulino, 1995).

[10] Ursula Coope, *Time for Aristotle: Physics IV.10–14* (Oxford: Clarendon Press, 2005).

[11] Tony Roark, *Aristotle on Time: A Study of Physics* (Cambridge: Cambridge University Press, 2011).

[12] Michael Bruder, "The Time of Our Lives: Aristotle on Time, Temporal Perception, Recollection, and Habituation." (McMaster University, 2011); Pierre-Luc Boudreault, "Aristotle's Account of Time: A Moderate Realism" (The University of Western Ontario, 2020).

[13] Andra Striowski, "Aristotle on Time and the Soul" (Ph.D. thesis, University of Ottawa, 2016).

[14] Chelsea C. Harry, *Chronos in Aristotle's Physics: On the Nature of Time* (London: Springer, 2015).

eternity in Plato, Aristotle etc,[15] a few ancient works by Themistius, Johannes Philoponus and Simplicius[16] as well as some modern commentaries.[17] Beyond these there are numerous publications that touch on or directly comment on aspects related to matters discussed in the ἀπορίαι.

Even though more or less all contributors explicitly recognise the ἀπορίαι in *Physics* IV.10 as precisely that, few of them actually treat them in this capacity, that is, as perplexing, humbling statements intended to wipe the slate clean to open up for new fresh thought in the direction of gaining new knowledge.[18] Except for differences in depth, detail and scope of previous studies of the ἀπορίαι, they can also roughly be placed along a cline ranging between two poles. The first pole represents a position where the ἀπορίαι are treated as Aristotle's precise and authoritative statements serving as a point of departure for the following enquiry into time, where the aporetic statements are more or less expected to seamlessly harmonise with Aristotle's following positive account, and the second pole represents

---

[15] Walter Mesch, *Reflektierte Gegenwart: eine Studie über Zeit und Ewigkeit bei Platon, Aristoteles, Plotin und Augustinus* (Frankfurt am Main: Klostermann, 2003).

[16] Themistius, *Themistius: On Aristotle Physics 4*, trans. Robert B. Todd, Ancient Commentators on Aristotle (London: Bloomsbury Publishing, 2003); Johannes Philoponus, *Philoponus: On Aristotle Physics 4.10–14*, trans. Sarah Broadie, Ancient Commentators on Aristotle (London: Bloomsbury Publishing, 2011) and Simplicius, *On Aristotle's Physics 4.1–5, 10–14*, trans. James O. Urmson, The Ancient Commentators on Aristotle (London: Duckworth, 1992). For a discussion on Simplicius' take on the 'now' in *Physics* IV.10, see Thomas Seissl Thomas Seissl, "Aristotle's "Now" and the Definition of Time: Method and Exegesis in Simplicius' Interpretation of Physics IV. 10," *History of Philosophy & Logical Analysis* 26, (2023): 366–386. Sorabji accounts for a few ancient thinkers whose work may have implications for the interpretation of the ἀπορίαι, such as Diodorus Cronus, Chrysippus, Poseidonius, Apollodorus, Alexander of Aphrodisias and Augustine (Sorabji, *Time, Creation and the Continuum: Theories in Antiquity and the Early Middle Ages*, 17–32).

[17] Aristotle, *Aristotelis Physica*, ed. W. D. Ross (Oxford: Clarendon Press, 1950 (repr. 1966) (1st edn. corr.)); Victor Goldschmidt, *Temps physique et temps tragique chez Aristote: Commentaire sur le Quatrième livre de la Physique (10–14) et sur la Poétique* (Paris: Librarie Philosophique J. Vrin, 1982); Edward Hussey, *Aristotle's Physics: Books III and IV, translated with notes by Edward Hussey* (Oxford: Clarendon Press, 1983); Luigi Ruggiu, *Aristotele: Fisica; saggio introduttivo, traduzione, note e apparati* (Milano: Rusconi Libri, 1995); Catherine Collobert, *Traité du temps: Physique, livre IV, 10–14* (Paris: Èdition Kimé, 2004), Laura M. Castelli, *Aristotele. Fisica. Libro IV.* (Roma: Carocci editore, 2012).

[18] David Bolotin, though, suggests that the ἀπορίαι are intended as a conscious challenge to the reader, "Aristotle has deliberately left work for us" (Bolotin, "Aristotle's Discussion of Time: An Overview", 47–48).

a complete rejection of the validity of the claims made in the ἀπορίαι. A further complication (to be discussed further in Sect. 5.1) is that the aporetic text body may be categorised in different ways in terms of structure and type, which also have implications for how they should (or could) be approached.

Attempting a rough sorting—which surely could be improved upon or fine-tuned—of the contributions to the study of the ἀπορίαι in *Physics* IV.10, we could in general terms categorise them as follows. At the first pole we find the ancient interpreters Simplicius[19] and Themistius,[20] as well as Andra Striowski who by building part of her analysis on the claims made in the ἀπορίαι consistently treats the ἀπορίαι as having a governing function where they are understood as factual statements that serve as a basis for the discussion of time that follows in the rest of Aristotle's chapters on time.[21] Hervé Barreau likewise indicates that he accepts the ἀπορίαι as they stand, stating as follows,

> Cette méthode consiste à partir des apories ou des problèmes les plus débattus, à essayer de les résoudre à l'aide d'analyses subtile ... C'est dans cette triple perspective qu'on va étudier les cinq chapitres du traité du temps, en suivant presque constamment l'ordre dans lequel se présentent les textes.
>
> This method consists in, starting from the aporiai or the most debated problems, trying to resolve them by means of subtle analyses ... It is from this triple perspective that we will study the five chapters of the treatise on time, almost consistently following the order in which the texts occur.[22]

Elena Cavagnaro–Stuijt's descriptive account of the ἀπορίαι is close to the first pole.[23] Norman Kretzmann is fairly close to the first pole, arguing that the ἀπορίαι are designed to counter "the familiar view that time is essentially, really *passing*."[24] Close to the first pole, at least in the formal sense, we also find Walter Mesch who never explicitly questions the validity of any of Aristotle's claims in his ἀπορία; he even states, "Auch die Vermutung, Aristoteles habe seine Zeitaporie gar nicht auflösen wollen,

---

[19] Simplicius, *On Aristotle's Physics 4.1–5, 10–14*, 696–700 (p. 102–107).
[20] Themistius, *Themistius: On Aristotle Physics 4*, 140,8–142 (p. 52–54).
[21] Striowski, "Aristotle on Time and the Soul", 51, 55, 58, 59, 60–65.
[22] Hervé Barreau, "Le traité aristotélicien du temps," *Revue Philosophique de la France et de l'Étranger* 163, (1973): 26; my translation.
[23] Cavagnaro-Stuijt, *Aristotele e il tempo: analisi di Physica, 4.10–14*, 30–48.
[24] Kretzmann, "Time Exists-but Hardly, or Obscurely", 92.

sondern nur zu zeigen versucht, daß sie auf verfehlten Voraussetzungen beruhe, vermag nicht zu überzeugen [Also the assumption that Aristotle did not want his time aporia to be resolved at all, but only tried to show that it depends on misdirected premises, is not convincing]."[25] However, he admits that the arrangement of the ἀπορίαι may be understood as "eine Zuspitzung"[26] and his fairly long and detailed discussion assumes a distancing from some of Aristotle's claims in the ἀπορίαι. Mesch notes that in spite of Aristotle's lucid discussion throughout his chapters on time, it remains "alles andere als klar [anything but clear]" *how* he resolves his ἀπορία.[27] Jon McGinnis is fairly close to the first pole by understanding the ἀπορίαι fairly positively[28] by reading them as "accounts that define time, and not as a general undefined concept."[29] To him they can be understood as "the logical space for a discussion of time," where "an account of time is either absolutist or relational, and either invokes temporal becoming or not."[30] Philoponus is less close to the first pole, rejecting Aristotle's claim that time does not exist.[31]

Ursula Coope is further away from the first pole, but is still fairly close.[32] However, her contribution is difficult to place along the cline in a proper sense, since she alternates between attempts to understand what Aristotle wants to say and her own position relative to the issues raised. She also argues against Aristotle's viewpoints even when they are corroborated by text passages outside the ἀπορίαι, in *Physics* IV.11–14 and passages drawn from the rest of *Physics*. Her approach has a value in itself for enquiring into the validity of Aristotle's claims but is less helpful if the purpose is to make sense of the meaning and function of the ἀπορίαι from the viewpoint that Aristotle expresses in his chapters on time and the *Physics* as a whole.

Somewhere in between the two poles but still closer to the first pole than the second, we find Jorge Torres. He understands the ἀπορίαι

---

[25] Mesch, *Reflektierte Gegenwart: eine Studie über Zeit und Ewigkeit bei Platon, Aristoteles, Plotin und Augustinus*, 369; my translation.
[26] Ibid., 370.
[27] Ibid., 359–385; my translation.
[28] McGinnis, "Making Time Aristotle's Way", 154.
[29] Ibid., 147.
[30] Ibid., 153.
[31] Philoponus, *Philoponus: On Aristotle Physics 4.10–14*, 702–708 (p. 3–10).
[32] Coope, *Time for Aristotle: Physics IV.10–14*, 17, 24; Chelsea Harry seems to partly argue along similar lines (Harry, *Chronos in Aristotle's Physics: On the Nature of Time*, 35, 40).

predominantly to be Aristotle's account of what he thinks time is *not*, thus not reflecting his positive conception of what time indeed *is* except for occasional elements also found in chapters 11–14.[33] He correctly notes that some claims in the ἀπορίαι will stand, being confirmed in subsequent chapters, "ellas se encargarán de adelantar algunas nociones fundamentales en relación a los desarrollos posteriores de la concepción aristotélica del tiempo (they [the ἀπορίαι] will form the basis for advancing some fundamental notions in relation to the later developments of the Aristotelian conception of time) [. . .] el punto inicial a partir del cual se despliegan todas las consideraciones posteriores de la investigación ([the ἀπορίαι are] the starting point from which all subsequent research considerations unfold)."[34] Other claims make up "un [. . .] punto de partida dispuesto a ser superado (a starting point that can be modified)," the non-existence of time belonging to that last category.[35] Somewhere in the middle we also find Nathanael Stein who argues in regard to the ἀπορία on the parts of time that

> we can give the puzzles raised by the *phainomena* a substantive response rather than one which seeks only a counterargument by which to justify rejecting their conclusion. ... I do claim that the puzzle warrants a response even by his [Aristotle's] own lights, and that the parts of his discussion on which I focus contain the grounds for a good response to the dialectical challenge of confirming or correcting our pretheoretical understanding of time. Further, those responses cohere with - and indeed appeal to - some of Aristotle's most fundamental conceptual innovations concerning natural science.[36]

Close to the second pole we find Richard Sorabji who asserts that Aristotle "certainly does not intend to accept them [the ἀπορίαι]."[37]

Close to, or even at, the second pole (of complete rejection of the ἀπορίαι) we find Tony Roark who argues that they are "bits of sophistic mischief whose tricks are easily identified when one properly understands

---

[33] Torres, "La aporética del tiempo: Un análisis reconstructivo de Fis. Δ 10, 217b29–218b20", 211.

[34] Ibid., 214; my translation.

[35] Ibid., 213.

[36] Stein, "Aristotle on Parts of Time and Being in Time", 499.

[37] Sorabji, *Time, Creation and the Continuum: Theories in Antiquity and the Early Middle Ages*, 7.

the nature of time"[38] and that they belong to the category of sophistical endoxa.[39] He does not offer much of an analysis, arguing that the third ἀπορία "is the only puzzle truly deserving of a proper solution,"[40] and then deals with it in not so many words. Roark ends his brief analysis commenting as follows, "To dispatch such seemingly deep puzzles as quickly as we have is perhaps less gratifying than straining to discover their solutions." To deal with them, Roark asserts, is "not only unnecessary, but also foolish," since they are only a "paper tiger."[41]

Such diverse distribution among contributors in regard to the assessment of the status and function of the ἀπορίαι in *Physics* IV.10 suggests that they reflect very different understandings of what an ἀπορία—particularly the ones in *Physics* IV.10—is, a subject we readily turn to now.

---

[38] Elsewhere Roark comments the introductory words of the first ἀπορία, "the discussion seems to go off course immediately" (Roark, *Aristotle on Time: A Study of Physics*, 43).

[39] Ibid., 43–44, 211; Nathanael Stein thinks a sophistic categorisation is a mistake, instead arguing that the first *aporia* constitutes a genuine philosophical question (Stein, "Aristotle on Parts of Time and Being in Time", 499, 518).

[40] Roark, *Aristotle on Time: A Study of Physics*, 213.

[41] Ibid., 215.

CHAPTER 3

The Concept of ἀπορία

Abstract *Aporia* has its beginning with Socrates and is either defined *subjectively* as a state of mind of being perplexed, at a loss or in a state of inarticulateness, or *objectively* as the cause and object of this state of mind—or the active correlation between the two. *Aporia* may also simply refer to an issue to be enquired into. An *aporia*, with two conflicting perspectives, may be presented by and/or represented within a single person, where the purpose of discussing and resolving the *aporia* is the development of science and the gaining of new knowledge. In a *negative aporia* the two opposing views both have to be rejected, whereas in a *positive aporia* two promising positions are pitted against one another—but only one can remain standing. The formulation of an *aporia* serves as a tool to precisely identify an issue to be enquired into, so that the core of the conundrum becomes visible—the purpose is to reach *euporia* 'a solution.' Failure to formulate an *aporia* may result in a situation where the enquirer does not know in which direction to go and may not even recognise whether the solution has been found or not, but the one who has specified the issue precisely will have a clear *telos* 'goal.'

Keywords Aporia • Euporia • Subjective *aporia* • Objective *aporia* • Topics • Negative *aporia* • Positive *aporia* • Plato • Meno • Socrates • Aporetic perplexity • Aporetic dissonance • Aporetic suffering

Ἀπορία figures both as a word and a concept. As a nominal lemma ἀπορία occurs some 250 times in the Aristotelian corpus, but there are also some 250 occurrences of its verbal form ἀπορέω that often co-occurs with its nominal form. Among its senses in Aristotelian usage we note 'to question something in a philosophical context,'[1] 'to be in doubt or express uncertainty'[2] and 'to put a philosophical question.'[3] Ἀπορία is the antonym of εὐπορία whose senses mirror those of ἀπορία: ease or facility (of doing something), a means of satisfying, assistance, abundance, plenty, welfare, advantages, wealth, solution of doubts or difficulties and resourcefulness.[4]

Ἀπορία as a concept begins with Socrates.[5] Ἀπορία, on the one hand, denotes a state of mind of being perplexed,[6] or, in the spirit of Plato, a state of inarticulateness and speechlessness[7] or being at a loss,[8] and, on the other, "the object and cause of this state of mind," where the first use often is understood as subjective whereas the second one is objective.[9] The cognitive state of ἀπορία is directed towards an object, a set of issues pre-

---

[1] Aristotle, *Analytica priora et posteriora*, ed. W.D. Ross (: 1964), 75a22–23: *to question* why one should ask for a concession of certain premises.

[2] Ibid., 82a18–19.

[3] Ibid., 90b1–2: raise a question as to whether it is equally possible to know a thing by definition and demonstration; Ibid., 98a35–36: raise a question in regard to cause and effect; Aristotle, *De anima*, ed. W.D. Ross (1961), 402b14–16: *a problem arising* as to whether objects corresponding to the functions should be considered before the parts themselves; Ibid., 408a34–b1: *raise a question* as to the movement of the soul.

[4] *LSJ* s.v. εὐπορ-ία, ἡ.

[5] Pierre Aubenque, "Sens et fonction de l'aporie socratique," *Philosophie antique. Problèmes, Renaissances, Usages* no. 3 (2003): 2–20, 7.

[6] Vasilis Politis, *The Structure of Enquiry in Plato's Early Dialogues* (Cambridge: Cambridge University Press, 2015), 134–135.

[7] George Karamanolis and Vasilis Politis, "Introduction," in *The Aporetic Tradition in Ancient Philosophy*, ed. George Karamanolis and Vasilis Politis, (Cambridge: Cambridge University Press, 2018), 1.

[8] In a dialogue in *Meno*, Meno complains that Socrates is "at a loss [ἀπορεῖς]" and "make[s] others to be at a loss [ἀπορεῖν]" and making him (Meno) "full of perplexity [ἀπορία]." In a discussion where a boy hit by Socrates' method, Socrates points to the usefulness of him "falling down into perplexity [ἀπορίαν]," inspiring him to go deeper into the enquiry and "benefit[ting] from being torpedoed." Socrates: "So note that in consequence of this perplexity [ἀπορίας] he will also find out [things] discovering [them] with me, while I [do] nothing else than asking and not teaching" (Plato, *Meno*, ed. J. Burnet (1903), 79c7–80a4, 84c4–d1). This is what Michael Erler would call the methodological aspect of ἀπορία, where it figures both as an end and "the new beginning for further searching" (Michael Erler, "Aporia," *Brill's New Pauly*, https://doi.org/10.1163/1574-9347_bnp_e128880 (accessed 28 October, 2017).

[9] Karamanolis and Politis, "Introduction", 2.

sented in the form of an ἀπορία, "that which generates the mental state [of ἀπορία]."[10] As for the aporetic state of mind Pierre Aubenque states, "L'aporie [est] … le sentiment d'inquiétude qui en découle [Aporia is the feeling of worry that stems from it "; it is "la situation psychologique qui en résulte [the psychological situation that results from it]."[11]

Karamanolis and Politis state, "the object to which this state of mind, aporia, is directed is likewise properly called an aporia."[12] What, on the whole, could be said to be lacking in Karamanolis and Politis' description of what constitutes an ἀπορία is awareness of the fact that ἀπορία as a term, at least in the Aristotelian corpus, is not only used about the exposition of irreconcilable contrasts, but also simply used in the sense of an *issue* to be discussed or investigated. There is thus a range from 'aporetic' in the strong sense to a much weaker sense.[13] Gareth Matthews argues that Aristotle, as opposed to Plato, is more concerned with ἀπορία as the object of enquiry that causes perplexity than the resulting mental state of ἀπορία.[14] More precisely one could argue that the *scope* of Aristotle's use of the term is wider, ranging from ἀπορία in the simple sense of 'an issue for discussion' to ἀπορία as a mental state of perplexity in the Platonic sense, as exemplified in Aristotle's discussion on ἀπορία in *Metaphysics* III.1 (see below). It is also noteworthy that in Aristotle's triple ἀπορία on time, there are ingredients bordering on the Platonic mental state of ἀπορία.

To Aristotle philosophy has its starting point in ἀπορία 'perplexity.'[15] As to the nature of the ἀπορία, Aristotle asserts in the *Topics* IV.6, that "the equality of contrary reasonings is a cause of perplexity [ἀπορία]";[16] ἀπορία is generated "*either* through generating a contradiction *or* through

---

[10] Ibid., 2, 6; Politis comments, "The aporiai in Plato's early dialogues are aporiai in the sense of the mental state of puzzlement and perplexity that results from one's search, in particular the search for the *ti esti* of a thing, having broken down and failed." (Politis, *The Structure of Enquiry in Plato's Early Dialogues*, 134–135).

[11] Aubenque, "Sens et fonction de l'aporie socratique", 8, 9; my translation.

[12] Karamanolis and Politis, "Introduction", 6; this double sense of the concept of ἀπορία is noted in Plato's Protagoras (Plato, *Protagoras*, ed. J. Burnet (1903), 324d–e).

[13] Cf. Cristina Rossitto's comment on the width of the use of ἀπορία as a methodological approach (Cristina Rossitto, *Studi sulla dialettica in Aristotele* (Napoli: Bibliopolis, 2000), 26).

[14] Gareth B. Matthews, *Socratic Perplexity and the Nature of Philosophy* (Oxford: Oxford University Press, 1999), 109.

[15] Ibid.

[16] Aristotle, *Topica*, ed. E. S. Forster, trans. E. S. Forster (1960), 605.

generating a compelling contradiction."[17] As opposed to a dialectical argument that involves competing parties or persons, an argument based on an ἀπορία may be presented by a single person and be *re*presented by "conflicts of reasons within one and the same person."[18] Christof Rapp argues that in the *Topics*, ἀπορία is used to qualify what Aristotle refers to as a 'dialectical problem,' which in its turn is equivalent to what Aristotle denotes as an ἀπορία in scientific and philosophical contexts.[19] This identification of ἀπορία with the dialectical problem is conducive to roughly restricting what qualifies as aporetic, not allowing ἀπορία to have too broad a range; though at the same time, one should not expect ἀπορίαι to conform to too strict a format.[20]

Aristotle uses 'dialectic' in three different ways in *Topics* I.2, referring to (i) training (γυμνάσια), (ii) the encounter with many, and (iii) philosophical sciences.[21] The last, which is our concern, can be subdivided into: (a) the going through of both sides of an ἀπορία, and (b) the provision of a method to discuss the principles applied to the sciences.[22] Rapp states "The dialectical method is useful for the philosophical sciences in that the philosophers can use certain aspects of this method in order to raise aporiai and in order to discuss principles of the different sciences on the basis of accepted opinions."[23] The ultimate purpose of discussing and resolving ἀπορίαι is the development of science[24] and the gaining of knowledge. McGinnis asserts that ἀπορίαι "may facilitate one's moving from a confused account about what some term signifies to a clearer and well articulated account about what the thing really is."[25] Pierre Aubenque argues that the ἀπορία is "le moteur du cheminement [the motor of the thought

---

[17] Karamanolis and Politis, "Introduction", 7.

[18] Ibid., 8; Politis, *The Structure of Enquiry in Plato's Early Dialogues*, 133–134.

[19] Christof Rapp, "Aporia and Dialectical Method in Aristotle," in *The Aporetic Tradition in Ancient Philosophy*, ed. George Karamanolis and Vasilis Politis, (Cambridge: Cambridge University Press, 2018), 112.

[20] Ibid., 112–113.

[21] Aristotle, *Topica*, ed. W. D. Ross (1960).

[22] Rapp, "Aporia and Dialectical Method in Aristotle", 115–116.

[23] Ibid., 116.

[24] Friedemann Buddensiek, "Aporia in Aristotle's Metaphysics B," in *The Aporetic Tradition in Ancient Philosophy*, ed. George Karamanolis and Vasilis Politis, (Cambridge: Cambridge University Press, 2018), 138.

[25] McGinnis, "Making Time Aristotle's Way", 146.

process]."²⁶ The use of iii.a is aptly described in *Topics* I.2, where διαπορῆσαι represents "to be at [a] loss, to be in the grip of a difficulty,"²⁷

> It is useful in relation to the philosophical sciences because if we have the ability to go through the difficulties (διαπορῆσαι) on either side we shall more readily discern the true as well as the false in any subject.²⁸

Aubenque²⁹ also points to the important passage in *Nicomachean Ethics* VII, where Aristotle states the following,

> Our proper course with this subject as with others will be to present the various views [τὰ φαινόμενα] about it, and then, after first reviewing the difficulties [διαπορήσαντας] they involve, finally to establish if possible all or, if not all, the greater part and the most important of the opinions generally held [τὰ ἔνδοξα] with respect to these states of mind; since if the discrepancies [δυσχερῆ] can be solved [λύσηταί], and a residuum of current opinion [τὰ ἔνδοξα] left standing, the true view will have been sufficiently established.³⁰

Friedemann Buddensiek notes that there are two principal ways of putting forth an ἀπορία; in both cases the core characteristic is that there is an insurmountable problem involved.³¹ First, 'the negative ἀπορία': in this case neither of the opposing viewpoints is acceptable *prima facie*—they must both be refuted because neither is viable. This type of ἀπορία presents "a double or two-sided problem."³² This kind of ἀπορία is exemplified in *Meno* as Socrates concludes that both the arguments that he has

---

²⁶ Aubenque, "Sens et fonction de l'aporie socratique", 8; my translation.
²⁷ Rapp, "Aporia and Dialectical Method in Aristotle", 117.
²⁸ Aristotle, *Aristotle. Topics. Books I and VIII. Translated with Commentary by Robin Smith* (Oxford: Oxford University Press, 1997), 101a34–36.
²⁹ Pierre Aubenque, "Sur la notion aristotélicienne d'aporie," in *Aristote et les problèmes de méthode: Communications présentées au Symposium Aristotelicum tenu à Louvain du 24 août au 1 Septembre 1960*, ed. Suzanne Mansion, ixtheo.de (Paris: Publications Universitaires de Louvain, 1980), 8.
³⁰ Aristotle, *Aristotle: The Nicomachean Ethics; a commentary by H. H. Joachim*, ed. D. A. Rees, (Oxford: Clarendon, 1951), VII.1.5; H. Rackhams's translation.
³¹ Buddensiek, "Aporia in Aristotle's Metaphysics B", 143; Karl-Heinz Iltinger offers the following definition: "eine unüberwindlich scheinende Schwierigkeit bei der Klärung wichtiger theoretischer Fragen, insbesondere wenn diese Schwierigkeit in der Form eines Widerspruchs auftritt, dessen These und Gegenthese aus anerkannten Grundsätzen bewiesen werden können" (Ilting, "Aporie", 110).
³² Buddensiek, "Aporia in Aristotle's Metaphysics B", 143.

proposed are inconclusive.[33] Second, 'the positive ἀπορία': here there are two quite (seemingly) defendable, opposing views, where both, however, cannot be accepted.[34] Politis particularly notes this kind of ἀπορία in the *Topics*.[35]

Metaphysics B (III), generally known as "il libro delle aporie [the book of aporias],"[36] is introduced by an enlightening account (995a24–995b2) regarding the usefulness of ἀπορίαι,

> Ἀνάγκη πρὸς τὴν ἐπιζητουμένην ἐπιστήμην ἐπελθεῖν ἡμᾶς πρῶτον περὶ ὧν ἀπορῆσαι δεῖ πρῶτον· ταῦτα δ' ἐστὶν ὅσα τε περὶ αὐτῶν ἄλλως ὑπειλήφασί τινες, κἂν εἴ τι χωρὶς τούτων τυγχάνει παρεωραμένον. ἔστι δὲ τοῖς εὐπορῆσαι βουλομένοις προὔργου[37] τὸ διαπορῆσαι καλῶς· ἡ γὰρ ὕστερον εὐπορία λύσις τῶν πρότερον ἀπορουμένων ἐστί, λύειν δ' οὐκ ἔστιν ἀγνοοῦντας τὸν δεσμόν, ἀλλ' ἡ τῆς διανοίας ἀπορία δηλοῖ τοῦτο περὶ τοῦ πράγματος· ᾗ γὰρ ἀπορεῖ, ταύτῃ παραπλήσιον πέπονθε τοῖς δεδεμένοις· ἀδύνατον γὰρ ἀμφοτέρως προελθεῖν εἰς τὸ πρόσθεν. διὸ δεῖ τὰς δυσχερείας τεθεωρηκέναι πάσας πρότερον, τούτων τε χάριν καὶ διὰ τὸ τοὺς ζητοῦντας ἄνευ τοῦ διαπορῆσαι πρῶτον ὁμοίους εἶναι τοῖς ποῖ δεῖ βαδίζειν ἀγνοοῦσι, καὶ πρὸς τούτοις οὐδ' εἴ ποτε τὸ ζητούμενον εὕρηκεν ἢ μὴ γιγνώσκειν· τὸ γὰρ τέλος τούτῳ μὲν οὐ δῆλον τῷ δὲ προηπορηκότι δῆλον.[38]

> It is necessary in reference to the sought-after [ἐπιζητουμένην] knowledge [ἐπιστήμην] that we first go over [the things] regarding which we must first raise difficulties [ἀπορῆσαι]. These are both all the things that some ones have perceived in different ways in regard to them, and if something except for these has happened to be overlooked. And for those wishing to gain clear knowledge [εὐπορῆσαι][39] it is convenient [προὔργου] to raise the difficulties [διαπορῆσαι] well. For the latter solution of difficulties is a solution [λύσις]

---

[33] Politis, *The Structure of Enquiry in Plato's Early Dialogues*, 169.

[34] Buddensiek, "Aporia in Aristotle's Metaphysics B", 143; regardless of which type of ἀπορία, one should note that the ἀπορία, as it is presented, may or may not include the term ἀπορία or one or several of its cognates; see also discussion by Enrico Berti (Enrico Berti, "Aristote et la méthode dialectique du Parmenide de Platon," *Revue internationale de philosophie* 34; 133/134, (1980): 341–358, 341–45.

[35] Politis, *The Structure of Enquiry in Plato's Early Dialogues*, 135.

[36] Cristina Rossitto, "La dialettica e il suo ruolo nella metafisica di Aristotele," *Rivista di Filosofia neo-scolastica* 85; /2/4, (1993): 370–424, 379; my translation. See also discussion on *Metaphysics* III by Javier Aguirre (Javier Aguirre, *Dialéctica y filosofía primera. Lectura de la Metafísica de Aristóteles* (Zaragoza: Prensas de la Universidad de Zaragoza, 2015), 41–59).

[37] Contraction of πρὸ ἔργου.

[38] Aristotle, *Metaphysica*, ed. W.D. Ross, 995a24–995b2.

[39] Or 'have their doubts resolved.'

of the earlier raised difficulties [ἀπορουμένων], but the ones ignorant of [ἀγνοοῦντας]⁴⁰ the bond are not [able] to untie [λύειν] it, but the perplexity [ἀπορία] of thought [διανοίας] makes this [bond] visible in regard to the matter [πράγματος]. For in so far as [ᾗ] [the mind] is puzzled [ἀπορεῖ], by this [puzzlement] it has suffered [something] nearly equal [παραπλήσιον] to those kept in bonds.⁴¹ For it is impossible to move forward in both ways.⁴² Therefore it is necessary to have observed all difficulties first, both on account of these things and because those who make enquiries without first raising the difficulties [διαπορῆσαι] are like those who do not know where they have to be going, and in addition to these [things], nor does one ever know whether one has found the thing sought for or not. For to this [man], on the one hand, the goal [τέλος]⁴³ is not clear, but, on the other, to the one who in advance has raised the difficulties [προηπορηκότι] it is clear.

This passage is of particular significance as Aristotle outlines his methodological approach to research.⁴⁴ Aristotle starts by underlining that in the quest for knowledge on a certain topic one needs to go through previously proposed perspectives as well related issues that may have been neglected in the enquiry, "It is necessary in reference to the sought-after [ἐπιζητουμένην] knowledge [ἐπιστήμην] that we first go over [the things] regarding which we must first raise difficulties [ἀπορῆσαι]. These are both all the things that some ones have perceived in different ways in regard to them, and if something except for these has happened to be overlooked." Regarding these, then, particular ἀπορίαι 'difficulties' need to be identified. The gaining of clear knowledge, εὐπορία, depends on a precise stating of these difficulties, "And for those wishing to gain clear knowledge

---

⁴⁰ Constructed with the accusative: 'to be ignorant of,' LSJ s.v. ἀγνο-έω I.

⁴¹ Or, 'enchained.'

⁴² In this translation Matthews proposes 'in both cases,' referring to the mind in an aporetic state and those imprisoned (Matthews, *Socratic Perplexity and the Nature of Philosophy*, 110); however, it seems more likely that Aristotle stays his course, focusing on the mind's aporetic struggle between two opposing proposals. Such an interpretation is supported by the immediately following comparison to the one who has acquainted himself with both sides in a legal matter (Aristotle, *Metaphysica*, 995b2–4). Politis also favours such an interpretation (Vasilis Politis, "Aristotle on Aporia and Searching in Metaphysics," in *Proceedings of the Boston Area Colloquium in Ancient Philosophy 18(1)*, (2003), 148–149).

⁴³ Or 'end' or 'purpose.'

⁴⁴ Leo Lugarini, *Aristotele e l'idea della filosofia*, 2 riveduta ed. (Firenze: La Nuova Italia, 1972), 143.

[εὐπορῆσαι]⁴⁵ it is convenient [προὔργου] to raise the difficulties [διαπορῆσαι] well." In support of his argument, he notes that the resolving of previous issues was the result of such specific identifications of the particular issues at hand.

He argues that enquirers into particular issues who do not bother to specify what the actual issues are will not be able to resolve them, "the ones ignorant of [ἀγνοοῦντας]⁴⁶ the bond are not [able] to untie [λύειν] it." Specifically, he argues that the contrasting of different options resulting in a mental state of ἀπορία, of inner conflict and cognitive challenge, serves the purpose of making the particular issues at hand visible, "the perplexity [ἀπορία] of thought [διανοίας] makes this [bond] visible in regard to the matter [πράγματος]." Aristotle describes the experience of the cognitive dissonance and mental effort resulting from ἀπορία as similar to the experience of people who are imprisoned. We should repeat that here ἀπορία refers to a mental state as opposed to ἀπορία in the sense of the difficulty itself. The reason for the deadlock is that while both sides of the ἀπορία, whether mentally or in terms of the /seemingly/ insurmountable problem one is faced with, still remain, "it is impossible to move forward." The similarity with ἀπορία in Plato's dialogues is striking, where ἀπορία as a mental state results from facing an obstacle within the enquiry and where the argument cannot move forward towards a successful completion.⁴⁷ However, put positively, the resolving of an ἀπορία results in εὐπορία, the resolving of the problem and the attaining and gaining of new knowledge.⁴⁸

To facilitate this forward motion, Aristotle underlines once again the importance of careful consideration of what the specific issues and difficulties are. Otherwise the enquirer risks not knowing in what direction to turn in his investigation and, moreover, with too vague a point of departure he may not even recognise whether the solution has been found or not,

---

⁴⁵ Or 'have their doubts resolved.'
⁴⁶ Constructed with the accusative: 'to be ignorant of,' LSJ s.v. ἀγνο-έω I.
⁴⁷ Politis, *The Structure of Enquiry in Plato's Early Dialogues*, 135.
⁴⁸ Ibid., 174.

Therefore it is necessary to have observed all difficulties first, both on account of these things and because those who make enquiries without first raising the difficulties [διαπορῆσαι] are like those who do not know where they have to be going, and in addition to these [things], nor does one ever know whether one has found the thing sought for or not.

Aristotle finally contrasts such as person who has an unclear goal (τέλος) with one who has gone through and identified the issues and who has a clear goal in mind, "For to this [man], on the one hand, the goal [τέλος][49] is not clear, but, on the other, to the one who in advance has raised the difficulties [προηπορηκότι] it is clear." To Aristotle the aporetic approach is particularly valid for metaphysical enquiries.[50]

---

[49] Or 'end' or 'purpose.'
[50] Politis, "Aristotle on Aporia and Searching in Metaphysics", 151.

CHAPTER 4

The ἀπορίαι in Physics 217b33–218a30

Abstract Aristotle asks whether time belongs to the category of things that exist or not, and argues that if it does its existence is so uncertain that it merits the question 'What then is it?' The enquiry into the *aporiai* requires a careful study and translation of the Greek text as a basis for a precise exegetical analysis. *Aporia* 1: Time is composed of past and future time. Time is always subjectively and cognitively perceived, a key point in Aristotle's thought on time that often is neglected. By the use of the optative δόξειε 'might seem' in regard to the issue as to whether time may partake in substance or not, Aristotle tentatively keeps the door open for such a possibility. *Aporia* 2: time, as opposed to objects in general, consists of non-existing parts. The 'now' (that does exist) is not a part. *Aporia* 3: The 'now' is presented as either the same 'now' or as a series of different 'nows.' Two 'nows' cannot co-exist nor can they follow one another back to back. The one and same 'now' in the extended sense cannot continue indefinitely; if so there would be no 'before' and no 'after,' and all things throughout history would co-exist. The 'now' is a divider of time. The limithood of the 'now,' constantly marking out the limit between past and future, is cognitively perceived.

Keywords Substance (Aristotle) • Aristotle's now • Part-whole • Same now • Different nows • Infinite now • Limithood

4.1 Introduction

The triple ἀπορία is preceded and followed by two statements, framing them so to speak. In his introduction of the discussion on time, Aristotle sets out to "raise difficulties [διαπορῆσαι] regarding it [time]." Here we should note the verb διαπορέω, a cognate of ἀπορία, which importantly signals that what follows belongs to the aporetic register.

> πρῶτον δὲ καλῶς ἔχει διαπορῆσαι περὶ αὐτοῦ καὶ διὰ τῶν ἐξωτερικῶν λόγων, πότερον τῶν ὄντων ἐστὶν ἢ τῶν μὴ ὄντων, εἶτα τίς ἡ φύσις αὐτοῦ. ὅτι μὲν οὖν ἢ ὅλως οὐκ ἔστιν ἢ μόλις καὶ ἀμυδρῶς, ἐκ τῶνδέ τις ἂν ὑποπτεύσειεν.[1]

> But first it is well to raise difficulties [διαπορῆσαι] regarding it [time][2] and on account of general arguments [ἐξωτερικῶν λόγων][3] whether [time] is [part] of the things existing [τῶν ὄντων] or the things not existing [τῶν μὴ ὄντων], then what its nature is. Therefore, that [time] either does not exist altogether or scarcely at all and obscurely, one might suspect from any of these [points].

Aristotle poses the two key questions, i.e. whether time could be said to belong to things existing or not, and if so, "what its nature is." These questions are not restricted to the particular enquiry into time, but are also part of Aristotle's overall research methodology when it comes to things whose existence may be in doubt, as indicated in *Posterior Analytics* II.1, where he asks two basic questions: εἰ ἔστιν . . . ἁπλῶς 'if it exists . . . *simpliciter*,' and if so, τί οὖν ἐστι 'what then is it'?[4] Aristotle's tentative conclusion almost puts into doubt the entire enquiry by its negative language as he points to the elusiveness of time.[5]

---

[1] Aristotle, *Physica*, ed. W.D. Ross, 217b30–33.

[2] Inserted for clarification and supplied from previous line.

[3] A bone of contention should be noted in the usage of the wording ἐξωτερικῶν λόγων which was puzzling even to ancient interpreters (Cavagnaro-Stuijt, *Aristotele e il tempo: analisi di Physica, 4.10–14*, 23–24); for an overview of the reception of ἐξωτερικοὶ λόγοι, see Ingemar Düring, *Aristotle in the Ancient Biographical Tradition*, Göteborgs Universitets Årsskrift, vol. LXIII (Stockholm: Almqvist & Wiksell, 1957), 426–443; see also discussion in Cavagnaro-Stuijt, *Aristotele e il tempo: analisi di Physica, 4.10–14*, 22–28.

[4] Aristotle, *Analytica priora et posteriora*, ed. W.D. Ross, 89b32–34.; cf. Cavagnaro-Stuijt, *Aristotele e il tempo: analisi di Physica, 4.10–14*, 29.

[5] Cf. Jacques Marcel Dubois, *Le temps et l'instant selon Aristote (Physic. IV, 10–14)* (Paris: Desclée de Brouwer, 1967), 136.

Right after the ἀπορίαι Aristotle sums up in a statement that does not offer much more hope for a positive outcome of his enquiry into time than his introductory words.

> τί δ' ἐστὶν ὁ χρόνος καὶ τίς αὐτοῦ ἡ φύσις, ὁμοίως ἔκ τε τῶν παραδεδομένων ἄδηλόν ἐστιν, καὶ περὶ ὧν τυγχάνομεν διεληλυθότες πρότερον.[6]

> But what time is and what its nature is, is similarly obscure both from what has been handed on [by earlier thinkers] and with regard to the things which we just now have gone through.

With these statements framing the ἀπορίαι, forming an *inclusio*, it is no surprise that the ἀπορίαι themselves often are referred to as Aristotle's negative account of time.

Aristotle's aporetic text in *Physics* IV.10 can be divided into three sections, or three ἀπορίαι.[7] The language of the ἀπορίαι is dense and marked by ellipsis. A precise translation is therefore significant for our prospects to grasp what Aristotle is arguing and as a basis for a precise exegesis of these aporetic passages. Below I offer the three texts in translation followed by analyses.

4.2 Ἀπορία 1: Physics 217b33–218a3

TEXT 1: τὸ μὲν γὰρ αὐτοῦ γέγονε καὶ οὐκ ἔστιν, τὸ δὲ μέλλει καὶ οὔπω ἔστιν. ἐκ δὲ τούτων καὶ ὁ ἄπειρος καὶ ὁ ἀεὶ λαμβανόμενος χρόνος σύγκειται. τὸ δ' ἐκ μὴ ὄντων συγκείμενον ἀδύνατον ἂν εἶναι δόξειε μετέχειν οὐσίας.[8]

For some of it has passed [γέγονε] and does not exist [ἔστιν], some is about to be [μέλλει] and does not yet exist [ἔστιν]. But of these both infinite [time] [ὁ ἄπειρος] and time [χρόνος] which always[9] is perceived[10]

---

[6] Aristotle, *Physica*, 218a31–33.
[7] Ibid., 217b33–218a30.
[8] Ibid., 217b33–218a3.
[9] Coope fuses ὁ 'what' and ἀεί 'always, ever' to 'whatever' in her translation, thus producing a sense not contained in the Greek. Or is she simply translating ὁ as 'whatever,' whatever the grounds may be for that, for then follows "on any given occasion" which might be a translation of ἀεί? The result is more of a paraphrase than a translation, which becomes problematic when basing her argument on such a loose foundation in her discussion further down. (Coope, *Time for Aristotle: Physics IV.10–14*, 18, 20).
[10] *LSJ* s.v. λαμβάνω, I.9.b: 'apprehend with the mind.' Chelsea C. Harry prefers the more literal gloss 'taken' as a translation (Harry, *Chronos in Aristotle's Physics: On the Nature of Time*, 33).

[ὁ ἀεὶ λαμβανόμενος]¹¹ are¹² composed. But what is composed of things that do not exist¹³ might seem [δόξειε] to be incapable of partaking of substance [οὐσίας].¹⁴

In our TEXT, ὁ ἄπειρος should most likely be understood as an ellipsis for ὁ ἄπειρος χρόνος 'infinite time'; if 'the infinite' had been intended

---

[11] Hussey paraphrases ὁ ἀεὶ λαμβανόμενος χρόνος as "any arbitrary time," which is much too imprecise (Hussey, *Aristotle's Physics: Books III and IV, translated with notes by Edward Hussey*, 41). Andra Striowski properly translates ἀεὶ λαμβανόμενος as 'always being grasped' (Striowski, "Aristotle on Time and the Soul", 50). Torres paraphrases ὁ ἀεὶ λαμβανόμενος χρόνος as 'el tiempo periódico [periodic time]' (Torres, "La aporética del tiempo: Un análisis reconstructivo de Fis. Δ 10, 217b29–218b20", 216); Catherine Collobert: "le temps indéfiniment périodique" (Collobert, *Traité du temps: Physique, livre IV, 10–14*, 17).

[12] Here the predicate σύγκειται agrees with the closest standing singular subject χρόνος, but since there are two subjects, 'are composed' is preferred.

[13] Instead of the more precise 'what is composed of things that do not exist,' Coope here translates τὸ δ' ἐκ μὴ ὄντων συγκείμενον as 'what is composed of non-beings' (Coope, *Time for Aristotle: Physics IV.10–14*, 18). Striowski follows Coope's translation literally (Striowski, "Aristotle on Time and the Soul", 50).

[14] Jon McGinnis renders οὐσία as 'being' (McGinnis, "Making Time Aristotle's Way", 148). Coope likewise translates οὐσία with 'being' (Coope, *Time for Aristotle: Physics IV.10–14*, 18). It seems Coope is following Hussey on this point (Hussey, *Aristotle's Physics: Books III and IV, translated with notes by Edward Hussey*, 41). Walter Mesch also understands οὐσία as having the sense 'Sein' (Mesch, *Reflektierte Gegenwart: eine Studie über Zeit und Ewigkeit bei Platon, Aristoteles, Plotin und Augustinus*, 365). Striowski translates 'beingness' (Striowski, "Aristotle on Time and the Soul", 50). Torres: 'la existencia' (Torres, "La aporética del tiempo: Un análisis reconstructivo de Fis. Δ 10, 217b29–218b20", 216). Sorabji: 'existence.' (Sorabji, *Time, Creation and the Continuum: Theories in Antiquity and the Early Middle Ages*, 8). Cavagnaro-Stuijt: 'sostanza' (Cavagnaro-Stuijt, *Aristotele e il tempo: analisi di Physica, 4.10–14*, 30). Collobert: 'l'etance' (Collobert, *Traité du temps: Physique, livre IV, 10–14*). Ruggiu's paraphrase translation does not translate οὐσία at all (Ruggiu, *Aristotele: Fisica; saggio introduttivo, traduzione, note e apparati*, 207). Castelli translates 'essere' (Castelli, *Aristotele. Fisica. Libro IV*, 97) and comments, "il riferimento alla "sostanza" in senso stretto non sembra appropriato" (Ibid., 201). However, both the immediate context (such as the immediately following second ἀπορία) and the overall context of the *Physics* would suggest that the more common translation of οὐσία as 'substance' would be more appropriate here. As will be demonstrated below in our analysis, the existence of time depends on its underlying thing, motion, which in turn has its seat in the moving thing, i.e. a substance.

Aristotle would have written τὸ ἄπειρον as he does in *Physics* 206a23.[15] When discussing the existence of time, Aristotle suggests that neither time that has gone by nor future time exists, "For some of it has passed [γέγονε] and does not exist [ἔστιν], some is about to be [μέλλει] and does not yet exist [ἔστιν]." On the other hand, it is precisely past and future time that are the constituents of time, whether we are talking about infinite time or the time that we always perceive, "But of these both infinite [time] [ὁ ἄπειρος] and time [χρόνος] which always is perceived [ὁ ἀεὶ λαμβανόμενος] are composed." Past and future time constitute both time as it infinitely stretches out in the direction of the past and the future, and time as it is constantly perceived by us, since the time we perceive continuously is manifested in the intersection between the past and the future. A key point here which might not strike the reader as significant at this introductory stage of Aristotle's analysis of time is the qualification of χρόνος, "which always is perceived." As noted further into Aristotle's discussion of time, perception is a significant ingredient in Aristotle's thought on time, and particularly time that is consistently perceived. 'Perception' suggests that the question of time is not reducible merely to a presumed mathematical fact but is contingent upon a variety of possible subjective-cognitive viewpoints on the part of the perceiver.

Having stated these two contradictory premises, Aristotle comes up with a tentative conclusion, suggesting that things—infinite time and time as we perceive it on a daily basis—that are composed of things without existence, may not be able to share in substance, "But what is composed

---

[15] Here Coope translates ὁ ἄπειρος as 'the infinite.' However, a few pages down she seems to be vacillating, referring to " 'infinite time' " in "the first puzzle." (Coope, *Time for Aristotle: Physics IV.10–14*, 18, 20). Striowski also translates 'the infinite,' but in her case it has more serious consequences because she builds her following argument on the understanding of ὁ ἄπειρος as strictly referring to 'the infinite' rather than to 'infinite time' (Striowski, "Aristotle on Time and the Soul", 50–57). This leads her in the wrong direction, such as in her interpretation of *Physics* 206a22–25 where Aristotle's discussion includes τὸ ἄπειρον (not to be confused with ὁ ἄπειρος [χρόνος] (Ibid., 52). Hussey gets it right here when he translates ὁ ἄπειρος as 'infinite time' (Hussey, *Aristotle's Physics: Books III and IV, translated with notes by Edward Hussey*, 41). Harry also understands ὁ ἄπειρος as an ellipsis where χρόνος is implied (Harry, *Chronos in Aristotle's Physics: On the Nature of Time*, 33, 36). Torres likewise: 'tiempo infinito' (Torres, "La aporética del tiempo: Un análisis reconstructivo de Fis. Δ 10, 217b29–218b20", 216); Elena Cavagnaro-Stuijt: 'il tempo illimitato' (Cavagnaro-Stuijt, *Aristotele e il tempo: analisi di Physica, 4.10–14*, 30). Sorabji: "infinite time" (Sorabji, *Time, Creation and the Continuum: Theories in Antiquity and the Early Middle Ages*, 8); Collobert, *Traité du temps: Physique, livre IV, 10–14*, 17: "le temps infini." The ancient interpreter Simplicius: "infinite time" (Simplicius, *On Aristotle's Physics 4.1–5, 10–14*, 696 (p. 104)).

of things that do not exist might seem [δόξειε] to be incapable of partaking of substance [οὐσίας]." Here we should importantly note the optative δόξειε 'might seem,' which indicates the tentativeness of this conclusion.

4.3 Ἀπορία 2: Physics 218a3–8

TEXT 2: πρὸς δὲ τούτοις παντὸς μεριστοῦ, ἄνπερ ᾖ, ἀνάγκη, ὅτε ἔστιν, ἤτοι πάντα τὰ μέρη εἶναι ἢ ἔνια· τοῦ δὲ χρόνου τὰ μὲν γέγονε τὰ δὲ μέλλει, ἔστι δ' οὐδέν, ὄντος μεριστοῦ. τὸ δὲ νῦν οὐ μέρος· μετρεῖ τε γὰρ τὸ μέρος, καὶ συγκεῖσθαι δεῖ τὸ ὅλον ἐκ τῶν μερῶν· ὁ δὲ χρόνος οὐ δοκεῖ συγκεῖσθαι ἐκ τῶν νῦν.[16]'

But in addition to these [things],[17] in regard to[18] any thing divisible [παντὸς μεριστοῦ], if it really exists, of necessity, when it exists, either all the parts or some exist. But in regard to[19] time [χρόνου], some [τὰ] [parts], on the one hand, have passed and some [τὰ] [parts], on the other, are about to be, but none exists, even though [time] is divisible. But the 'now [νῦν]' is not a part. For the part [τὸ μέρος] measures [the whole], as well as it is necessary that the whole is composed of the parts. But time [χρόνος] does not seem to be composed of 'nows [νῦν].'

In this short paragraph, Aristotle contrasts what could be said about most other items with time as a general category and another time category, the 'now.' Aristotle starts by arguing that any divisible thing, if it exists (and that is a key point here), has parts. These parts, or at least some of them, exist, "But in addition to these [things], in regard to any thing divisible [παντὸς μεριστοῦ], if it really exists, of necessity, when it exists, either all the parts or some exist." In contrast, when it comes to time, even though it is divisible, none of its parts exists since the parts of time either belong to the past or the future, "But in regard to time [χρόνου], some [τὰ] [parts], on the one hand, have passed and some [τὰ] [parts], on the other, are about to be, but none exists, even though [time] is divisible."

---

[16] Aristotle, *Physica*, 218a3–218a8.

[17] Coope does not translate πρὸς δὲ τούτοις at all (Coope, *Time for Aristotle: Physics IV.10–14*, 19), whereas Hussey translates this prepositional phrase with 'further' (Hussey, *Aristotle's Physics: Books III and IV, translated with notes by Edward Hussey*, 41). Castelli's translation is closest to the Greek, 'Oltre a queste cose ['Besides these things']' (Castelli, *Aristotele. Fisica. Libro IV*, 97).

[18] Literally 'of.'

[19] Literally 'of.'

Here it should be noted that time indeed has parts, even though it is here argued that they do not exist, a problem to be dealt with further ahead in my discussion.[20]

Aristotle continues, arguing that the 'now' is not a part of time, "But the 'now [νῦν]' is not a part." Aristotle explains why: a part is the measure of the whole and, viewed from the other way around, the whole is made up by the parts, "For the part [τὸ μέρος'] measures [the whole], as well as it is necessary that the whole is composed of the parts." Aristotle concludes, "But time [χρόνος] does not seem to be composed of 'nows [νῦν].' "

4.4   Ἀπορία 3: Physics 218A8–30

TEXT 3: ἔτι δὲ τὸ νῦν, ὃ φαίνεται διορίζειν τὸ παρελθὸν καὶ τὸ μέλλον, πότερον ἓν καὶ ταὐτὸν ἀεὶ διαμένει ἢ ἄλλο καὶ ἄλλο, οὐ ῥᾴδιον ἰδεῖν.[21] εἰ μὲν γὰρ αἰεὶ ἕτερον καὶ ἕτερον, μηδὲν δ' ἐστὶ τῶν ἐν τῷ χρόνῳ ἄλλο καὶ ἄλλο μέρος ἅμα (ὃ μὴ περιέχει, τὸ δὲ περιέχεται, ὥσπερ ὁ ἐλάττων χρόνος ὑπὸ τοῦ πλείονος), τὸ δὲ νῦν μὴ ὂν πρότερον δὲ ὂν ἀνάγκη ἐφθάρθαι[22] ποτέ, καὶ τὰ νῦν ἅμα μὲν ἀλλήλοις οὐκ ἔσται, ἐφθάρθαι δὲ ἀνάγκη ἀεὶ τὸ πρότερον. ἐν αὐτῷ μὲν οὖν ἐφθάρθαι οὐχ οἷόν τε διὰ τὸ εἶναι[23] τότε, ἐν ἄλλῳ δὲ νῦν ἐφθάρθαι τὸ πρότερον νῦν οὐκ ἐνδέχεται. ἔστω γὰρ ἀδύνατον ἐχόμενα εἶναι ἀλλήλων τὰ νῦν, ὥσπερ στιγμὴν στιγμῆς. εἴπερ οὖν ἐν τῷ ἐφεξῆς οὐκ ἔφθαρται ἀλλ' ἐν ἄλλῳ, ἐν τοῖς μεταξὺ [τοῖς] νῦν ἀπείροις οὖσιν ἅμα ἂν εἴη· τοῦτο δὲ ἀδύνατον. ἀλλὰ μὴν[24] οὐδ' αἰεὶ τὸ αὐτὸ διαμένειν δυνατόν· οὐδενὸς γὰρ διαιρετοῦ πεπερασμένου ἓν πέρας ἔστιν, οὔτε ἂν ἐφ' ἓν ᾖ συνεχὲς οὔτε ἂν ἐπὶ πλείω· τὸ δὲ νῦν πέρας ἐστίν,

---

[20] Mesch jumps to conclusions when he in regard to the second ἀπορία claims, "Demnach ist die Gegenwart streng genommen ein punktuelles Jetzt"; as Aristotle indicates in the third ἀπορία the 'now' is merely a limit (Mesch, *Reflektierte Gegenwart: eine Studie über Zeit und Ewigkeit bei Platon, Aristoteles, Plotin und Augustinus*, 365).

[21] Torres translates, "Además, no es fácil ver si el "ahora", que parece separar (διορίζει) el pasado (τὸ παρελθόν) y el futuro (τὸ μέλλον), permanece (διαμένει) siempre uno y el mismo, o es siempre otro diferente (Furthermore, it is not easy to see if the "now", which seems to separate (διορίζει) the past (τὸ παρελθόν) and the future (τὸ μέλλον), remains (διαμένει) always one and the same, or is always something different) (Torres, "La aporética del tiempo: Un análisis reconstructivo de Fis. Δ 10, 217b29–218b20", 228).

[22] LSJ s.v. ἀνάγκη, 1. ἀνάγκη ἐστί, c. inf.

[23] Here διὰ τὸ εἶναι is used as causal modifier (Evert van Emde Boas and others, *The Cambridge Grammar of Classical Greek* (Cambridge: Cambridge University Press, 2019), 604).

[24] LSJ s.v. μήν: II.3.

καὶ χρόνον ἔστι λαβεῖν πεπερασμένον.²⁵ ἔτι εἰ τὸ ἅμα εἶναι κατὰ χρόνον καὶ μήτε πρότερον μήτε ὕστερον τὸ ἐν τῷ αὐτῷ εἶναι καὶ ἑνὶ [τῷ] νῦν ἐστιν, εἰ τά τε πρότερον καὶ τὰ ὕστερον ἐν τῷ νῦν τῳδί ἐστιν, ἅμα ἂν εἴη τὰ ἔτος γενόμενα μυριοστὸν τοῖς γενομένοις τήμερον, καὶ οὔτε πρότερον οὔτε ὕστερον οὐδὲν ἄλλο²⁶ ἄλλου.²⁷

But yet, the 'now [τὸ νῦν]'—which seems to separate the past [τὸ παρελθὸν] and the future [τὸ μέλλον], whether the one and the same always persists[28] or is one after another[29]— is not easy to discern. For if there always is another and then another, none of the [τῶν] [nows] is in time, one part [μέρος] after the other, at the same time [ἅμα] (which [ὃ] [part] does not encompass [another part], but the [τὸ] [part] is encompassed, just as the shorter time by the longer [time]),[30] and [if] the former 'now [νῦν]' does not exist [μὴ ὄν] but it is necessary at some time to have been destroyed, [then] also the 'nows [τὰ νῦν]' will not exist with one another at the same time [ἅμα], but it is always necessary for the former ['now'] to have been destroyed. So, in itself, on the one hand, [the former 'now'] has not been able to be destroyed because it at that time existed, but, on the other, it is not possible for the former 'now' to be destroyed in another 'now.' For let it be impossible for the 'nows [τὰ νῦν]' to cling to one another,[31] just as a point to a point. Therefore, if indeed [the 'now'] has not been destroyed in the [τῷ] ['now'] next to it, but in another [one], it would exist at the same time in the boundless 'nows' in between. But this is impossible. Yet truly the same ['now'] is not able always to continue.[32] For nothing divisible that is finite has *one* limit, whether it would be continuous in one [direction] or more. But the 'now' consists[33] [ἐστίν] of a limit, and it is possible to perceive time as brought to a limit [πεπερασμένον]. Yet if the 'being' [τὸ [. . .] εἶναι] is at the same time according to time and is neither a 'before [πρότερον]' nor an 'after [ὕστερον],' the 'being [τὸ [. . .] εἶναι] is in the same and in the one 'now'; if both the 'befores [τά [. . .] πρότερον]' and the 'afters [τὰ ὕστερον]'

---

[25] Here ἔστι . . . πεπερασμένον is a periphrasis (Ibid., 198).
[26] Regarding ἄλλο ἄλλου, see Ibid., 359.
[27] Aristotle, *Physica*, 218a8–218a30.
[28] Or 'continues.'
[29] LSJ s.v. ἄλλος, II.3: 'one thing after another.'
[30] Philoponus argues that e.g. two days cannot occur together, but a day may occur in a month (Philoponus, *Philoponus: On Aristotle Physics 4.10–14*, 703 (p. 4). Simplicius argues along similar lines (Simplicius, *On Aristotle's Physics 4.1–5, 10–14*, 698 (p. 105).
[31] *LSJ* s.v. ἔχω, C.1.
[32] Or 'persist.'
[33] *LSJ* s.v. εἰμί, C.II.b.

are in this 'now [νῦν],' the things that took place 10,000 years ago might be at the same time with the things that took place today, and neither is there a 'before [πρότερον]' nor an 'after [ὕστερον],' no one different than the other [ἄλλο ἄλλου].

The third ἀπορία is by far the longest of the three and is focused on the nature of the 'now.' The elusive 'now' is what distinguishes between time that has gone by and future time, "the 'now [τὸ νῦν]'—which seems to separate the past [τὸ παρελθὸν] and the future [τὸ μέλλον]." Aristotle then, in a topic sentence, introduces the two themes that will be dealt with in the rest of the ἀπορία, the 'now' as the identical entity that always continues as it extends, or the 'now' as a type with many tokens, 'nows' lining up, following one another, "whether the one and the same always continues or is one after another."

Starting with the 'now' understood as 'nows' following one another, Aristotle first notes that with this understanding, 'nows' would not be in time at the same time, "For if there always is another and then another, none of the [τῶν] [nows] is in time, one part [μέρος] after the other, at the same time [ἅμα]." The 'part' is here understood as a reference to the 'now,' or rather, a series of 'nows' appearing in a succession, though none of them ever being in time at the same time. In his parenthetical comment, Aristotle substantiates this claim by pointing out that a 'part', a 'now,' cannot encompass another 'now,' i.e., they cannot occur at the same time. Instead, it is encompassed by something that is more than a 'now,' in the same manner as more time includes less time, "which [ὃ] [part] does not encompass [another part], but the [τὸ] [part] is encompassed, just as the shorter time by the longer [time]." As Aristotle continues, he points out that a 'now' that has passed does not exist anymore because at some point it must perish, "the former 'now [νῦν]' does not exist [μὴ ὄν] but it is necessary at some time to have been destroyed." This is why a 'now' will not co-exist with another 'now,' "the 'nows [τὰ νῦν]' will not exist with one another at the same time [ἅμα], but it is always necessary for the former ['now'] to have been destroyed." The question is when a 'now' is destroyed. It may not be destroyed during its existence, "So, in itself, on the one hand, [the former 'now'] has not been able to be destroyed because it at that time existed, but, on the other, it is not possible for the former 'now' to be destroyed in another 'now.'" Aristotle underlines that 'nows' cannot intrude on one another's existence, "For let it be impossible for the 'nows [τὰ νῦν]' to cling to one another, just as a point to a point." Just like a point cannot follow immediately upon another point, a 'now' cannot follow directly upon another 'now,' since a 'now' is without extension and merely consists in a limit, "But the 'now' consists[34] [ἐστίν] of a limit." Further, Aristotle elaborates on what the consequences would be if we would allow 'nows' to transcend their limits, "Therefore, if indeed [the 'now'] has not been destroyed in the [τῷ] ['now'] next to it, but in another [one], it would exist at the same time in the boundless 'nows' in between." Aristotle concludes: "But this is impossible."

To summarise, if 'nows' are thought to follow upon one another under the following premises,

(i) 'nows' following upon one another cannot be in time at the same time
(ii) 'nows' following upon one another cannot exist at the same time, but the former 'now' must be destroyed before the next 'now'
(iii) a 'now' cannot be destroyed in another 'now,' neither in the next 'now' nor in any other 'now'
(iv) 'nows' cannot cling to one another, i.e., be immediately next to one another, for 'nows' do not have any extension since a 'now' is only a limit,

then 'nows' cannot follow one another.

Turning to the second possibility, that of understanding the 'now' as continually ongoing, Aristotle outright states that the one and same 'now' cannot keep going for ever, "Yet truly the same ['now'] is not able always to continue." To support his argument, he contrasts the 'now' with what holds true for any finite object, namely that each object has more than one limit, "For nothing divisible that is finite has *one* limit, whether it would be continuous in one [direction] or more." Objects of the world are characterised by their finiteness and divisibility. Continuous objects have limits that define them, and they may be divided infinitely many times. In contrast, the 'now' is neither an extended object nor a part of such an object. In contrast with divisible, finite objects, the 'now' not only *has* only one limit, but it *is* a limit, "But the 'now' consists[35] [ἐστίν] of a limit, and it is

---

[34] *LSJ* s.v. εἰμί, C.II.b.
[35] *LSJ* s.v. εἰμί, C.II.b.

possible to perceive time as brought to a limit [πεπερασμένον]." The function of the 'now' is to be the divider of time, setting a limit for time, between past and present; its 'limithood' is the defining characteristic of 'now.'[36] Here we should also note the sense of λαβεῖν whose sense may be to 'apprehend with the mind'[37]—abbreviated to 'perceive' in our translation—which sense would be quite in agreement with several arguments throughout Aristotle's five chapters on time where he points to the centrality of the perceiving mind for the identification, definition, understanding and even the existence of time as he understands it. This suggests that "to perceive time as brought to a limit [πεπερασμένον]" is not just something said in passing, but most likely refers to the cognitive perception of the 'now' and its function as a demarcation of both an end and a beginning.

The last lines of the third ἀπορία deal with the consequences that would follow if we would not accept the claim that each 'now' has a limit (and *is* a limit). If we would allow the 'now' to continue, all 'being' would be at the same time, Aristotle argues, resulting in there being neither a 'before' nor an 'after,' but the 'being' would reside in that everlasting 'now,' "Yet if the 'being' [τὸ [. . .] εἶναι] is at the same time according to time and is neither a 'before [πρότερον]' nor an 'after [ὕστερον],' the 'being [τὸ [. . .] εἶναι] is in the same and in the one 'now.' " With such an understanding, Aristotle elaborates, things occurring long time ago would be at the same time as those happening today, since any 'before' or 'after' would coincide in time, "if both the 'befores [τά [. . .] πρότερον]' and the 'afters [τὰ ὕστερον]' are in this 'now [νῦν],' the things that took place 10,000 years ago might be at the same time with the things that took place today." In fact, there would not be a 'before' or an 'after' to be distinguished as separate entities in time, "neither is there a 'before [πρότερον]' nor an 'after [ὕστερον],' no one different than the other [ἄλλο ἄλλου]."

The main point of Aristotle's discussion of the continuous and eternally extending /lasting 'now' is that he outright rejects it. Our task now, in the following sections, is to see how we can make sense of the ἀπορίαι.

---

[36] Cf. Barreau: "son rôle est celui d'une limite [its role is that of a limit] (Hervé Barreau, "L'instant et le temps selon Aristote (Physique IV, 10–14, 217b29–224a17)," *Revue philosophique de Louvain* 66, (1968):, 214); my translation.

[37] Aristotle, *Topica*, λαμβάνω, I.9.b.

CHAPTER 5

Identifying the Aporetic Contrasts

Abstract *Aporias* are basically either negative *aporiai* or positive ones, though the *aporiai* in *Physics* IV.10 mostly are negative ones. The structure of the *aporias* may be understood in different ways, either as two or three *aporias*, or even as one large *aporia*. They may also be understood as three-step rocket, building on one another. Neat, clearcut *aporias* are rare; in *Physics* IV.10 only the third *aporia* may be categorised as such. Even though the text practically speaking can be divided into three *aporias*, several aporetic contrasts can be identified across them, where a claim in one *aporia* contrasts with or connects to a claim in another *aporia*.

A number of aporetic contrasts may be identified, as follows. Aporetic contrast 1: Aristotle's questioning of time's existence, listing several persuasive arguments, is contrasted against the *endoxa*, the opinion of the general public or the opinion of the informed elites. Aporetic contrast 2: The location of existing time would either have to be in past or future time, or in the 'now,' but Aristotle outright rejects both these proposals. Aporetic contrast 3: Implied in the aporetic material is the contrast between a cognitive-subjective perspective on time and one that is more mathematical and matter-of-fact. Time is, on the one hand, always perceived, whether empirically or cognitively, and dependent on a subjective perceiver for its passing, or even existence. On the other hand, past and future time and the 'now' are at the same time approached as units in a logical and mathematical economy. Aporetic contrast 4: A major issue in

© The Author(s), under exclusive license to Springer Nature Switzerland AG 2024
J. H. Nylund, *Resolving Aristotle's Aporia on Time*,
https://doi.org/10.1007/978-3-031-65010-9_5

Aristotle's discussion on time is the relation of time to substance, that is, whether time is able to be a partaker of substance or not. This is a key issue in view of the fact that time is part of Aristotle's physics. Time's connection to 'being,' and therefore potentially to substance, is implied at the same time as it is suggested that non-existents (past and future time) may not be able to take part in substance. Aporetic contrast 5: The 'now' may either be taken to be a part of time or not; its potential parthood is suggested but mostly denied. Aporetic contrast 6: 'Nows' are presented as multiple tokens of a type, following one another, and, in contrast, a single 'now' is posited as the one and same 'now' that expands and for ever continues. Since 'nows' cannot occur in a series back-to-back, and since a 'now' cannot be the same in the sense of including all events throughout history, thus nullifying the notion of a 'before' and an 'after,' Aristotle rejects both options.

Keywords Aporetic contrast • Existence of time • Non-existence of time • Endoxa • Eternal now • Infinite past • Past time • Future time • Cognition (Aristotle) • Subjective time • Objective time • Time as substance • Ousia • Part(s) of time • Now as part • Parthood • Same now • Different nows • Serial nows • Eternal now

5.1 Introduction

As we noted in Chap. 3, the defining characteristic of an ἀπορία is the presence of irreconcilable contrasts, whether real or apparent ones. As stated earlier, there are basically two kinds of ἀπορίαι: negative ἀπορίαι and positive ἀπορίαι. That our text mostly belongs to the former category is not surprising as it is often referred to as Aristotle's negative account of time. In the case of a negative ἀπορία, both sides of the argument must be rejected and replaced by a better alternative, whereas a positive ἀπορία involves opposing views that both seem defendable, but where both cannot be true at the same time and some kind of alteration of the argument must be made to arrive at *one* viable option.

When we consider our aporetic text (*Physics* 217b33–218a30), it is not entirely self-evident how to structure the material. One could argue that what decides how we divide this chunk of text is the correlation between what holds certain lines of text together thematically and what connects, or rather, attracts them to other units of text. Here we could borrow two terms from chemistry: *cohesion* and *adhesion*, where cohesion is the power that holds something together internally and adhesion is the power that would gravitate parts or the whole of that coherent unit towards another text unit or part/s of text. For instance, it would make good sense to divide the text into three ἀπορίαι[1] as we have done (Chap. 4) because they discuss certain topics. However, one could also argue that the first ἀπορία could be seen as one unit together with what is normally referred to as the second ἀπορία because they raise similar issues. Another way to approach the text would be to say that it is made up of a chain or that it is a three-step rocket where certain elements in the first ἀπορία connects to certain elements in the second ἀπορία and certain elements in the second ἀπορία lead on to elements in the third ἀπορία. Alternatively, we could understand the text as one large ἀπορία because there are themes across the whole text that contrast with one another. These concerns could properly be said to belong to the field of discourse analysis.

These issues have bearing on how we apply ἀπορία as a concept. In the strict, idealised sense, an ἀπορία is a text chunk where two opposing, irreconcilable views are spelled out and clearly pitted against one another. This neat version of an ἀπορία does not really materialise in our aporetic text except in the third ἀπορία. Moreover, in our aporetic text there are not only contrasts within these ἀπορίαι but there may also be an aporetic contrast between a claim in one ἀπορία and a claim in another one. This complicates the picture, because there are, on the one hand, good reasons to delineate three distinct ἀπορίαι at the same time as there are, on the other, equally good reasons to pay attention to contrasting claims across the whole text. This presence of 'local' aporetic contrasts in the organised, delineated sense as well as 'global' aporetic contrasts across the whole text makes the analysis and interpretation more complex. The global aporetic contrasts, being less explicit, are not as readily consciously detected but certainly add to the intuitive sense of the reader that something 'fishy' is going on, that something 'just doesn't add up.'

To account for this complexity, I have chosen to address both local and global aporetic contrasts. That is, I am attempting to identify aporetic contrasts regardless of how we structure the text; this is some kind of catch-all-strategy whose rationale seems reasonable since the presence of

---

[1] Such as preferred by Walter Mesch (Walter Mesch, "Zeit," in *Aristoteles Handbuch: Leben - Werk - Wirkung,* ed. Christof Rapp and Klaus Corcilius, (Berlin: J.B. Metzler Verlag, 2021), 463.

irreconcilable contrasts between opposing positions is the overriding and defining characteristic of an ἀπορία. We are also, pragmatically speaking, concerned to resolve all and any aporetic tensions that we can detect in our text regardless of how and where they manifest in the text. 'Aporetic contrast' then fittingly widens the sense of ἀπορία, catering to the fact that the aporetic in our text only exceptionally comes in a neat, well-structured format and is rather mostly contextually and organically conditioned.

In the following subsections (Sects. 5.2–5.7), I identify aporetic contrasts throughout *Physics* 217b33–218a30, and in Chap. 6, I attempt to work out how these contrasts can be resolved.

5.2 The Existence or Non-existence of Time

The first and most basic aporetic contrast is the one between the observed and intuitive certainty of any reader that time indeed exists,[2] and Aristotle's provocative insistence in the first ἀπορία that time probably does not exist at all. This argument is launched already in the topic sentence introducing the triple ἀπορία, just before the first ἀπορία,

ὅτι μὲν οὖν ἢ ὅλως οὐκ ἔστιν ἢ μόλις καὶ ἀμυδρῶς, ἐκ τῶνδέ τις ἂν ὑποπτεύσειεν.[3]

Therefore, that it [time] either does not exist altogether or scarcely at all and obscurely, one might suspect from any of these [points].

In terms of type of ἀπορία, one could here argue that it is a positive ἀπορία since the arguments put forth by Aristotle in regard to the non-existence of time, on the one hand, and the common understanding of time as existent, on the other, both are persuasive, and since one of them will remain standing. This kind of aporetic contrast is unusual in the sense that the opposing contrast is not expressed at all, but its contrast is so obviously anchored in the *endoxa* that there is no need to account for this view. In the *Topics,* Aristotle defines *endoxa* as follows,

---

[2] Cf. Sorabji, *Time, Creation and the Continuum: Theories in Antiquity and the Early Middle Ages,* 7: "Any purposive agent must have a rudimentary idea of the difference between the future desired state of affairs and the present actual state [. . .] he must have some crude awareness of time, and any being capable of considering the existence of time is likely to be a purposive agent." See also Ibid., 13.

[3] Aristotle, *Physica,* 217b32–33.

Those are endoxa on the other hand, which seem so to everyone, or to most people, or to the wise – to all of them, or to most, or to the most famous and esteemed.[4]

In regard to the existence of time the *endoxa* would be the established opinion of "everyone, or [. . .] most people."

In the first ἀπορία, Aristotle highlights what might put into question whether time truly exists. First, the fact that the elements of time—the past and the future—do not exist, since the past is already gone and the future has not yet come, might be a problematic circumstance for the one arguing for the existence of time. Second, if the components of time do not exist it might be hard to argue that they may partake in substance (οὐσία). Three, in the second ἀπορία Aristotle brings attention to the fact that what constitutes any divisible thing is that all or some of its parts exist. Time, though divisible, cannot be said to consist of existing parts. Four, as for the 'now' that possibly would be the remaining candidate to make up a component of time, Aristotle bluntly states that it "is not a part," and since 'parthood' is a defining characteristic of existing things, neither does the 'now' qualify as a basis for arguing in favour of the existence of time. Five, in the last line of the second ἀπορία he asserts that time does not seem to be composed of 'nows.'

By these arguments Aristotle offers thorough evidence for the non-existence of time[5] and brings the readers to some kind of zero-point, where his audience cannot but nod approvingly: time by this description does not exist. Kretzmann notes similarly that "One might therefore feel justified, if uncomfortable, at this stage in saying that time does not exist."[6] Yet, this conclusion stands in stark contrast to the intuitive and experienced facticity of time on the part of any reader, that is, the *endoxa* of "everyone, or [. . .] most people."[7] By that same logic of Aristotle's neither would journeys exist since neither the distance already made nor the one not yet made strictly speaking exists, but few would accept the claim

---

[4] Aristotle, *Aristotle. Topics. Books I and VIII. Translated with Commentary by Robin Smith*, I. 10, 104 8–12; Jonathan Barnes understands τὰ ἔνδοξα as 'the reputable things [*or* views]' (Jonathan Barnes, "Aristotle and the Methods of Ethics," *Revue internationale de philosophie* 34; 133/134, (1980): 490–511, 500).

[5] Cf. Themistius who after having gone through all three ἀπορίαι concludes that "it can be established that time does not exist" (Themistius, *Themistius: On Aristotle Physics 4*, 142 (p. 54)).

[6] Kretzmann, "Time Exists-but Hardly, or Obscurely", 98.

[7] Cf. Philoponus, *Philoponus: On Aristotle Physics 4.10–14*, 702 (p. 3).

that journeys do not exist; when the same claim is applied to time it may be perceived to be more acceptable because time is a more abstract and less tangible category, which, of course, Aristotle capitalises on in the formation of this aporetic contrast.

5.3 Time as Infinite Past and Future or Eternal 'Now'

Closely related to the issue of the existence of time is the sub-issue of where existing time might be located, whether in past or future time (the first ἀπορία) or in an eternal 'now' (the third ἀπορία).

In the first ἀπορία, Aristotle willingly accepts that time is composed of past and future, only they do not exist because the past is gone, and the future is not yet here. In the third ἀπορία, Aristotle discusses whether there is an eternal 'now' that for ever extends throughout time. If there were an eternal 'now,' those things that took place 10,000 years ago would be contemporaneous with things happening today, a notion that Aristotle sharply rejects. Instead, he argues that the 'now' is merely a limit between past and future with no extension at all and which therefore does not exist. Both sides of this negative aporetic contrast, either of locating time in the infinite past and future or in an eternally extended 'now,' are rejected.

5.4 Time as a Cognitive-Perceptive or Logical Category

In Aristotle's aporetic exposition we may note a contrast between a cognitive-subjective perspective, on the one hand, and one where the argument is made on the basis of some kind of mathematical, matter-of-fact necessity, on the other. Neither side of this aporetic contrast is explicitly spelled out in our aporetic text but both are implied. This aporetic contrast, which could be classified as the equivalent to a negative ἀπορία, has been a continuous bother to interpreters and commentators (though not in the conscious sense of an aporetic contrast).

In the first ἀπορία, Aristotle talks about time as a category "which always is perceived." This wording brings to our attention three things. First, that time as category is related to, and even dependent on, our perception of it (as Aristotle argues elsewhere[8]). This claim might seem to be

---

[8] Aristotle, *Physica*, 223a25–28.

based on too meagre a basis if all there were is a possible sense of the word λαμβάνω, but since Aristotle multiple times throughout his five chapters on time in more explicit terms connects time and its existence to perception, it seems safe to maintain that this is how we should understand λαμβάνω in this text, and to understand it in the strong, specific sense that finds support elsewhere. The use of λαμβάνω in this sense is also found in the third ἀπορία, "it is possible to perceive [λαβεῖν] time as brought to a limit." Second, if we accept the gloss for λαμβάνω as 'apprehend with the mind,' this verb also lexicalises a reference to the mind, which suggests dependence on the subjective workings and perspective of the mind in the perception of time, which claim also finds support elsewhere in Aristotle's chapters on time. Third, ἀεί 'always' is a key to more than what perhaps is obvious to the eye at this point and in this short passage, but Aristotle elsewhere[9] makes an argument that time's existence is dependent on our *constant* perception of it, which means that at moments where 'always' is not upheld, that is, when we do not consciously detect and are aware time, time does not fully exist.

As for the mathematical perspective, Aristotle's entire exposition—in contrast to these cues to cognitive-subjective reflection—of the problems (ἀπορίαι) related to time, is marked by and communicated in a strict matter of fact style. For instance, the argument towards proving the non-existence of time in the first ἀπορία has the character of the strict rigour necessary to convince the readers of the validity of the line of argumentation. The same can be maintained about Aristotle's argument against the 'now' or 'nows' as components of time in the second ἀπορία and the argument put forth in regard to the nature of the 'now' in the third ἀπορία.

The contrast between the implied cognitively and subjectively based perspective, on the one hand, and that of Aristotle's matter of fact style where the workings of time emanate from the necessity of strict logic, on the other, leaves the reader with an unresolved contrast, torn, like Buridan's ass, between two potentially equally attractive alternatives.

5.5 Time as Partaker of Substance or Not

Yet another aporetic contrast highlighted by Aristotle is the one between time as a category partaking of substance and one where time cannot partake of substance. Against the background of the *Physics* as a whole this is a pivotal issue.

[9] Ibid.

At the end of the first ἀπορία Aristotle tentatively states that the constituents of time—the past and the future—do not seem to have a share of οὐσία [substance], "things that do not exist might seem [δόξειε] to be incapable of partaking of substance [οὐσίας]." As noted before, several commentators suggest οὐσία be translated as 'existence' or 'being' or something similar. In contrast to the first ἀπορία, at the end of the third ἀπορία Aristotle talks about the 'being'—which is the topmost category in Aristotle's system of 'being' of which οὐσία is a subcategory—of the 'before' (the past) and the 'after' (the future), "Yet if the 'being' [τὸ [. . .] εἶναι] is at the same time according to time and is neither a 'before [πρότερον]' nor an 'after [ὕστερον],' the 'being [τὸ [. . .] εἶναι] is in the same and in the one 'now.'" So, here it is assumed that the past (the 'before') and the future (the 'after') have a 'being.' Whether the constituents of time partake of substance/'being' or not is thus uncertain as Aristotle at the one point suggests that the parts of time may not be able to share in substance and at the other assumes that they have a 'being.'

The contradictory arguments bring the reader to a point of standstill as there does not seem to be any solid ground on this issue. This ἀπορία may be categorised as a positive ἀπορία.

5.6 'Nows' as the Parts of Time or Not

In this aporetic contrast, both the possibility of 'nows' as the parts, i.e. components, making up time, and a denial of such a possibility figure.

At the end of the second ἀπορία the reader is left with the inconclusive but suggestive wording that "time [χρόνος] does not seem to be composed of 'nows [νῦν].'" A couple of lines before Aristotle has stated, "But the 'now [νῦν]' is not a part [of time]." But then, at the beginning of the third ἀπορία, the 'now' is again in focus and its potential extension and possible parthood and multiplicity throughout time is actualised in the mind of reader, raising the hope that there after all is some solid ground in the 'now' as a part of time. A few lines down in the third ἀπορία, when Aristotle is discussing 'nows' as tokens of a type, he refers in explicit terms to 'nows' as parts, "none of the [τῶν] [nows] is in time, one part [μέρος] after the other, at the same time [ἅμα]." Here it seems, after all, that 'nows' are parts of time. In the following parenthesis that offers an elaborating comment, a reference to 'nows' as parts is again repeated (though elliptically so), "(which [ὅ] [part] does not encompass [another part], but the [τὸ] [part] is encompassed, just as the shorter time by the longer

[time])." However, as the reader keeps reading, these hopes are shattered as it turns out that the 'now' after all is argued not to be that point of departure for such an understanding that might have been hoped for.

Regardless whether this aporetic contrast between assuming and denying the parthood of the 'now' is conscious or not on the part of Aristotle, it is a contrast that needs resolving. This aporetic contrast may be categorised as a positive ἀπορία.

5.7 The 'Now' as Different or Same

The aporetic contrast in the third ἀπορία, where the 'now' as 'different' ones and 'the same' are contrasted, is in fact the only typically structured ἀπορία of our aporetic text; both sides of this negative ἀπορία will have to be rejected. The opposing sides are the contrast between an understanding of the 'now' as an ever-expanding/extended entity and one where the 'now' is understood as a multiplicity of 'nows,' following one another as tokens of a type.

In the third ἀπορία, as accounted for in detail above, Aristotle points to the difficulty of discerning the nature of the 'now.' Discussing 'nows' as tokens of a type, Aristotle presents several premises for such an understanding of 'now,' reaching the conclusion that such an understanding of the 'now' must be rejected. 'Nows' as tokens of a type are contrasted by the understanding of the 'now' as a single expanding/extended 'now,' i.e. the one and the same 'now' is understood as continual without an end. This, though, is problematic because that would be an eternal 'now' where there would be no 'before' or 'after,' where things taking place long time ago would be contemporaneous with today's events. It is obvious that Aristotle rejects this understanding of the 'now' too.

The reader is left with two contradictory alternatives, the 'now' as different and the 'now' as same, in regard to the nature of the 'now,' none of which is accepted by Aristotle.

CHAPTER 6

Resolving the Aporetic Contrasts in Context

Abstract Section 6.1: 'Aporia' refers both to a state of mind of being perplexed and the object and cause of this state of mind. Aristotle points to the need of making aporetic contrasts in issues up for discussion explicit. Once an *aporia* is made explicit it serves as a tool to establish what is true and what is false, and to find an *euporia* 'a solution.' In order to be able to assess the claims of the *aporias* in *Physics* IV.10 the entire book of *Physics* needs to be consulted.

Section 6.2: A key question in regard to the existence or non-existence of time is how to understand ἐστιν 'is, exists.' In a discussion of τὸ εἶναι 'being' and ἐστιν in the sense of 'exists,' Aristotle distinguishes between potential and actual existence of time, so that past and future time exists potentially and have or will exist actually at the point of the 'now' as illustrated by the occurrence of the Olympic Games. From a cognitive perspective Aristotle acknowledges the so-called *experienced* 'now' that clusters around the actual extension-less 'now,' where the experienced 'now' stretches in either or both directions from the 'now' as far as pragmatically convenient. Past and future time may also be approached from the viewpoint of cosmic time where their potential existence may be categorised as non-present existence rather than as non-existence; in hylomorphic terms their 'being' is thus 'being' *qua* qualified. The 'now' is not a part and time does not consist of 'nows.' Time is that which is between two 'nows.' Time cannot exist, or even be perceived, without the 'now.'

© The Author(s), under exclusive license to Springer Nature Switzerland AG 2024
J. H. Nylund, *Resolving Aristotle's Aporia on Time*,
https://doi.org/10.1007/978-3-031-65010-9_6

45

Section 6.3: As for the location of existing time, both the infinite past/future and the 'now' both were rejected in the ἀπορία. Nevertheless, Aristotle argues that the 'now' is the basis for the existence of time; just like there would be no time without the 'now,' there would be no 'now' without time.

Section 6.4: Time is presented from two perspectives: one where the 'now' is an abstract mathematical limit and one where time and the 'now' are perceived from a cognitive-perceptive point of view as experienced entities. The empirical observation of time and the internal, subjective experience of time as a phenomenon dovetail; reason and perception towards a cognitive conceptualisation join forces. Time is taken to have passed when it has been physically perceived or even just cognitively imagined. When a 'before' and 'after' are *perceived*, there is time. Time does not exist without a perceiving mind, except in a very restricted sense.

Section 6.5: Time has 'being' without itself being a substance by its correlation to an underlying thing that partakes in substance. The underlying thing of time is motion and motion takes place and manifests in a moving thing, a substance. Time and motion are mutually dependent on one another; though time depends more on motion (than vice versa) and motion depends on magnitude/space. Time and motion operate together both in potentiality and actuality. Time numerates and measures the underlying motion of the moving thing. By cosmic time there is a precise correlation between time and motion in space. The sun is the underlying constantly moving substance of time, and specifically the 'now.' Time partakes of substance by being a quality of the motion of a moving thing, a substance, i.e. the sun.

Section 6.6: Time is not composed of 'nows.' Nor is there an extended 'now.'

Section 6.7: The one and the same 'now' is both the same and different; it is the same by persisting in its passing, it is different by its accidental newness in each new position along its path. In its differentness the 'now' divides time in potentiality. In its sameness as a moving 'now' it unites past and future in actuality. It is thus the same 'now' that divides and unites; as a potential divider it is qualitatively different, as an actual uniter it is qualitatively the same. The 'now' travels through time in its actuality and divides time in its potentiality and is therefore 'different' in its 'being' in one position relative to another along the temporal axis.

Keywords Perplexity • *Aporia* as mental state • *Aporia* as object of enquiry • *Euporia* 'resolution' • Solution of problem • Aporetic contrast • Cognitive dissonance • *Metaphysics* III.1 • *Topics* I.2 • Finding the truth • 'Being' • Potential time • Actual time • Experienced 'now' • Non-present existence • Symbiosis of time and the now • Infinite time • Mathematical now • Logical now • Cognitive now • Cognitive-perceptive now • Subjective now • Perception of time • Before and after • Substance • Time as partaker of substance • Motion as underlying thing • Potentiality • Actuality • Cosmic time • Moving substance • Sun as moving substance • Extended now • Now as same • Now as different • Sameness • Differentness • Travelling time • Potentiality (Aristotle) • Actuality (Aristotle)

6.1 Introduction

As noted before (Chap. 3), ἀπορία refers both to a state of mind of being perplexed and at a loss, and to the object and cause of this state of mind. The subjective state of perplexity and confusion is caused by the set of issues presented in the form of an ἀπορία or an aporetic contrast. The latter category of aporetic contrasts may be perceived at some level but not necessarily consciously recognised by readers and analysts, but certainly experienced. They have the potential of causing cognitive dissonance, a sense of a suffering "nearly resembling those kept in bonds," to use Aristotle's wording in *Metaphysics* III.1 in regard to the mental state of ἀπορία. In this passage we noted Aristotle's strong recommendation that issues up for discussion be made explicit by identifying aporetic contrasts.

The ἀπορίαι and the aporetic contrasts that we have identified have the capacity, as argued by Aristotle in *Topics* I.2, to be useful as a means to "discern the true as well as the false in any subject" as we endeavour "to go through the difficulties (διαπορῆσαι) on either side." The goal is "a solution [λύσις] of the earlier raised difficulties [ἀπορουμένων]," to reach an εὐπορία 'resolution,' as Aristotle asserts in *Metaphysics* III.1. Aubenque comments that when there is more than one answer to a question the questioner is left with the obligation to make a choice.[1]

Our task now is to find out what the status is of the claims made in the ἀπορίαι and to work out what is false and what is true in regard to these

---

[1] Aubenque, "Sens et fonction de l'aporie socratique", 9.

claims, and what might be kept in a modified form. To be able to make this assessment we have to widen our circle of reference points by including and consulting both the immediate context of Aristotle's five chapters on time and the broader context of the full volume of the *Physics* in regard to what Aristotle's view really is on the issues raised in the three ἀπορίαι, to establish whether they can be corroborated or should be rejected or whether they must be further nuanced and elaborated on.[2] Stein favours such an approach when he argues that Aristotle would want us to find "responses that start from problems and then alter or refine our understanding of the relevant issues, in such a way as to remove confusion while preserving what was correct in the *phainomena*."[3]

In Sects. 6.2–6.7, the six ἀπορίαι/aporetic contrasts raised in Sects. 5.2–5.7 are tentatively placed in context for this purpose.

6.2 In Context: The Existence or Non-existence of Time

A key difficulty in the discussion of the existence of time is the usage of the verb ἐστιν 'is, exist' and its cognates with their potential meanings. Coope discusses loosely the possibility of time having an atemporal existence, though she dismisses, both at the beginning and end of her discussion, that Aristotle would accept such a solution.[4] Roark is on the right track when he argues that Aristotle[5] in the first ἀπορία on the existence of time treats "an accidental characterisation of time as an essential characterisation, and then erroneously draws conclusions about the very existence of time based on this accidental characterisation." That is, Roark is right about the distinction between accidental and essential characterisations of time, but not about his claim that Aristotle (unawares) draws the wrong conclusion; here we should assume, in the light of what we can gather from what he says elsewhere in *Physics*, that he is constructing an ἀπορία with a certain agenda in mind, as we argued in the introduction.

---

[2] Ideally, we should consult the whole Aristotelian corpus, but within the scope of this study that is too much to include.

[3] Stein, "Aristotle on Parts of Time and Being in Time", 500.

[4] Coope, *Time for Aristotle: Physics IV.10–14*, 19–21.

[5] Roark refers pejoratively to the writer of the first ἀπορία as "the puzzle monger," perhaps reflecting his claim that the ἀπορίαι (the third ἀπορία in particular) perhaps somehow are coloured by or even originate from a sophistic context (Roark, *Aristotle on Time: A Study of Physics*, 211–212).

6 RESOLVING THE APORETIC CONTRASTS IN CONTEXT

Unfortunately, Roark does not offer much further analysis as to what the implications of his observation might be, but simply rejects the definition of time in the first ἀπορία.[6]

The problem of 'being' was noted early on. As commented in *Physics* 185b, Lycophron even banned the word 'is' due to the difficulties it involved.[7] In the first ἀπορία, ἐστιν no doubt means 'exist,' but the possible meanings of 'is' (ἐστιν) pave the way for more than one possible meaning. In *Physics* 206a, Aristotle discusses its nominalised form, τὸ εἶναι 'being,' and ἐστιν in the sense of 'exists,'

ἀλλ' ἐπεὶ πολλαχῶς τὸ εἶναι, ὥσπερ ἡ ἡμέρα ἔστι καὶ ὁ ἀγὼν τῷ ἀεὶ ἄλλο καὶ ἄλλο γίγνεσθαι, οὕτω καὶ τὸ ἄπειρον (καὶ γὰρ ἐπὶ τούτων ἔστι καὶ δυνάμει καὶ ἐνεργείᾳ· Ὀλύμπια γὰρ ἔστι καὶ τῷ δύνασθαι τὸν ἀγῶνα γίγνεσθαι καὶ τῷ γίγνεσθαι).[8]

But since the 'being' [τὸ εἶναι] is in many ways, just as the day is and the national games [ὁ ἀγὼν][9] are by the becoming of one thing after another always, so is also the infinite [τὸ ἄπειρον] (for in regard to these, [the 'being'] is both in potentiality [δυνάμει] and in actuality [ἐνεργείᾳ]. For the Olympic Games exist; the games [τὸν ἀγῶνα] are both to take place in potentiality [τῷ δύνασθαι] and in the [actual] taking place [τῷ γίγνεσθαι]).

In connection to infinite [time],[10] Aristotle underlines that τὸ εἶναι 'the being' "is in many ways." 'Being' or 'existence' can thus be understood in different senses. To resolve the difficulty regarding in what sense different parts of a time period truly exist (or 'are'), he introduces the difference between *potentiality* and *actuality*. With reference to a part of a time period, such as a day of a month or a particular event taking placing during a period of time, he illustrates the difference between the *potential* existence of all the parts of, for instance, the Olympic Games, and what is *actualised* at a certain moment, "for in regard to these [i.e. the day and the

---

[6] Ibid., 212.

[7] Aristotle, *Physics*, ed. Jeffrey Henderson, trans. Philip H. Wicksteed & Francis M. Cornford (1929), 25.

[8] Aristotle, *Physica*, 206a21–25.

[9] Literally 'the contest,' but since it is evident in context that ὁ ἀγὼν refers to the Olympic Games I have translated 'the national games.'

[10] I am not suggesting that τὸ ἄπειρον 'the infinite/unlimited' here is short for ὁ ἄπειρος [χρόνος] as in the first ἀπορία, but the context still suggests that the discussion is about time placed in the broader context of infinity and therefore specifically infinite time.

Olympic Games],[11] [the 'being'] is both in potentiality [δυνάμει] and in actuality [ἐνεργείᾳ]." The Olympic Games *as a whole* exist only *potentially*—but they do exist—whereas each part, one at a time, during the actualisation process, exists *actually*, "For the Olympic Games exist; the games [τὸν ἀγῶνα] are both to take place in potentiality [τῷ δύνασθαι] and in the [actual] taking place [τῷ γίγνεσθαι])." Striowski misses the point when she argues as follows,

> We have just seen that time as composed of past and future fails to provide a sense of its active 'happening' that can be grasped as another and another in the manner of the day or games [. . . .] Since the now is not a part of time, it does not allow us to circumvent the difficulty of explaining how the time that we are always grasping must be composed of the past and the future.[12]

Instead it is precisely because the 'now' is constantly actualised[13] that there *is* past and future time in potentiality; the parts of time, i.e. the past and the future, owe their existence as parts of time to the constant actualisation of the 'now' that makes up the continuous limit between past and future time. In this passage Aristotle talks about parts of a day being actualised, one part at a time, which admittedly is considerably more in terms of extension than the non-extended 'now' that merely serves as a limit between past and present. The implied reference to parts of the day being actualised as it progresses deviates from Aristotle's understanding of the 'now' in the strict, mathematical sense. However, one could argue that this passage captures the tension between the 'now' as a limit and the 'now' as what we could term the *experienced* 'now' that—focused around the 'now' as a limit—at the cognitive level extends somewhat in either or both directions from the extension-less 'now' into the past and the future.[14] Aristotle discusses the *experienced* 'now' in *Physics* IV.13.[15] The 'now' is, as it were, dependent on "the proximity of the event to the strict,

---

[11] My clarification.

[12] Striowski, "Aristotle on Time and the Soul", 58.

[13] Contra Seissl (and Simplicius) who argues that to consider time by referring to the 'now' "is to grasp time only in its potentiality." (Seissl, "Aristotle's "Now" and the Definition of Time: Method and Exegesis in Simplicius' Interpretation of Physics IV. 10", 381).

[14] See Sorabji for partly similar thoughts (Sorabji, *Time, Creation and the Continuum: Theories in Antiquity and the Early Middle Ages*, 12–14).

[15] Aristotle, *Physica*, 222a20–22.

durationless now."[16] Here we can draw on insights from cognitive science and cognitive linguistics. The perception of the 'now' and time by way of bodily experience could be said to be conceptualised through *visual scanning*[17] so that the passing of time represented by motion in terms of *conceived time* gets a cognitive representation.[18] With a so-called *sequential scanning* of the 'now,' attention is turned to its continual passing, whereas with a *summary scanning* the passing 'nows' are conceptualised in such a way that a *Gestalt* whole is assembled,[19] so that an extension in time is cognitively conceptualised. A number of similarities between Aristotle's account and ideas within cognitive science and cognitive linguistics can be noted, or otherwise put, Aristotle's thought on time issues anticipates developments within cognitive sciences, such as psychology and neuroscience, as well as cognitive linguistics, disciplines that did not have their beginnings until the 1970s onwards. We will have reason to draw on such insights in the continued analysis below.

However, we can also start from the broader perspective, the cosmological dimension of time that Aristotle, similarly to Plato in the *Timaeus*,[20] discusses and commits to in *Physics* IV.14, where it is argued that time ultimately is based on the motion of the universe, such as indicated by the sun.[21] Such an understanding is well anchored in the collective embodied mind where time clearly connects to the perceived (but not real) motion of the sun in the correlation between the self and world.[22] The parts of time that exist potentially could be said to be part of cosmic time. Here the 'now' may be perceived in terms of *Gestalt* psychology as the *figure* in a figure-ground segregation, where past and future time constitutes the

[16] Inwood, "Aristotle on the Reality of Time", 158.

[17] Ronald W. Langacker, "Cognitive Grammar," *The Oxford Handbook of Linguistic Analysis*, https://doi.org/10.1093/oxfordhb/9780199677078.013.0005, 112.

[18] Vyvyan Evans and Melanie Green, *Cognitive Linguistics: An Introduction* (Edinburgh: Edinburgh University Press, 2006), 535.

[19] Friedrich Ungerer and Hans-Jörg Schmid, *An Introduction to Cognitive Linguistics* (Harlow: Longman, 1996), 191–192; Evans and Green, *Cognitive Linguistics: An Introduction*, 535.

[20] See Plato, *Timaeus* (Bury), 37c6-d7.

[21] Harry errs when she reduces Aristotle's raising of "the unchanging movement of the heavens" in *Physics* VIII to merely the function of a preparation for the upcoming discussion in *De caelo* (Harry, *Chronos in Aristotle's Physics: On the Nature of Time*, 37) On this point, see also Stein's discussion on Aristotle's commitment to cosmic time (Stein, "Aristotle on Parts of Time and Being in Time", 501, 505, 509–10, 517).

[22] Cf. Bolotin (Bolotin, "Aristotle's Discussion of Time: An Overview", 52, -54).

ground and the 'now' is foregrounded,[23] has *Prägnanz*, i.e. prominence, as it were.[24] In the terminology of Stein, time that exists potentially, i.e. past and future time that has existed or will exist, could be categorised as having *non-present existence* rather than belonging to the category of *non-existence*. Stein argues that Aristotle would probably argue that "events are composed of a past and future which somehow meet at the now. Since their pasts and futures are not nonbeings in the strict sense, there is no commitment to the absurdity of attempting to compose being out of two strict nonbeings."[25] In hylomorphic terms, a distinction can be made between 'being' *simpliciter* and 'being' *qua* qualified,[26] where this understanding is further strengthened. Stein asserts that past and future

> are not times or states of affairs or events that exist at times other than the present, but that either once did or will in the future exist in the present. Rather, they are past and future states of continuously existing underlying subjects, which may or may not be the states they have now. ... the temporal distinctions introduced by the now are not equivalent to ontological distinctions among what exists now, what will exist, and what has existed, but rather to distinctions among the ways in which subjects are now, the ways they have been, and the ways they will be.[27]

Within this framework the usage of the difference between potential and actual existence, past, present and future time can thus all be said to exist in some sense, whether actually or potentially, which resolves the seeming problem of non-existing time (Sect. 5.2, point 1). This also solves the problem of time consisting of non-existing parts (Sect. 5.2, point 3), since all its parts all exist either actually or potentially; as for time's *actual* existence it seems to be intended on the part of Aristotle to be understood in terms of past and future time's immediate association with the adjacent, absolute 'now.' Present and actual time is thus the time immediately prior to and after the 'now' that by association with the 'now' is taken to be

---

[23] Jan H. Nylund, "The Prague School of Linguistics and its Influence on New Testament Language Studies," in *The Language of the New Testament. Context, History, and Development*, ed. Stanley E. Porter and Andrew W. Pitts, Linguistic Biblical Studies (Leiden/Boston: Brill, 2013), 213, 216.

[24] Ungerer and Schmid, *An Introduction to Cognitive Linguistics*, 32–33.

[25] Stein, "Aristotle on Parts of Time and Being in Time", 513.

[26] Ibid., 514–15, 517.

[27] Ibid., 515–516.

actual. There is thus a negotiation between the notion of time in strict, mathematical terms and the notion of time as a cognitive entity based on the actual perception of time where the present is the temporal space extending on either side of the absolute 'now,' again, as discussed by Aristotle in *Physics* IV. 13 where the 'now' is allowed to extend as far in both directions from the absolute 'now' as the perceiver find it pragmatically convenient. Inwood similarly notes the contrast between "Aristotle's austerely mathematical conception of time and the phenomenology of our temporal experience, to which he often appeals."[28] Actual, present time thus clusters around the absolute 'now.' This interpretation should not be taken as a last resort to save the day for time as an actually existing entity, but rather as Aristotle's complementary understanding, where the mechanics of time, on the one hand, are understood in mathematical terms, but, on the other, as a cognitive reality depending on the perception of the mind, as discussed in some detail in Sect. 6.4.

However, when it comes to Aristotle's assertions that the 'now' is not a part (Sect. 5.2, point 4) and that time is not composed of 'nows' (Sect. 5.2, point 5), these claims seem to hold water, being corroborated several times. In *Physics* 237a, Aristotle states, "but in the 'now' there is no change."[29] Coope does not seem to be aware of this passage,[30] for she states, "The argument I have given assumes that it is possible for something to be changing now. It is possible, that is, to be changing at the instant that is the boundary between the past and the future."[31] However, she refers to a similar passage in *Physics* 234a24–3 that has been used to show that Aristotle denies that change can take place in a 'now.' In the first two lines it is explicitly stated, "That nothing can move in the 'present now,' the following considerations will show . . ." [32] (or literally, 'But that nothing moves in the 'now,' . . . [ὅτι δ' οὐθὲν ἐν τῷ νῦν κινεῖται, . . .[33]]).

---

[28] Inwood, "Aristotle on the Reality of Time", 167.

[29] Aristotle, *Physica*, 237a11–15: ἔτι δ' εἰ τὸ συνεχῶς μεταβάλλον καὶ μὴ φθαρὲν μηδὲ πεπαυμένον τῆς μεταβολῆς ἢ μεταβάλλειν ἢ μεταβεβληκέναι ἀναγκαῖον ἐν ὁτῳοῦν, ἐν δὲ τῷ νῦν οὐκ ἔστιν μεταβάλλειν, ἀνάγκη μεταβεβληκέναι καθ' ἕκαστον τῶν νῦν· 'But still if that which is changing continuously and was not destroyed, nor have ceased from change it must either change or have changed in any one ['now'] – but in the 'now' there is no change – it must have changed according to each of the 'nows.'" (my translation).

[30] At least this passage is not listed in her Index Locorum of passages that she discusses (Coope, *Time for Aristotle: Physics IV.10–14*, 185).

[31] Ibid., 26.

[32] Aristotle, *Physics*, 121.

[33] Aristotle, *Physica*, 234a24–25.

Coope argues that ἐν may either be translated as 'in' or 'at.' Drawing on the context of the following lines, she dismisses Owen's proposed translation[34] of ἐν τῷ νῦν κινεῖται as 'is changing *at* [a 'now']*,*' thus preferring ἐν τῷ νῦν to be translated '*in* the 'now.' '[35] Coope's argument is solid but really gets her nowhere since she does not present any argument as to how the statement ὅτι ... οὐθὲν ἐν τῷ νῦν κινεῖται 'that ... nothing moves *in* a 'now' ' could support her assertion that something *does* change in a 'now,' especially since Aristotle ends the passage by concluding, οὐκ ἄρα ἔστιν κινεῖσθαι ἐν τῷ νῦν 'Therefore, there is no motion in the 'now.' '[36]

If there is no change in a 'now,' there is no change in several 'nows,' which means that 'nows' cannot be parts of time; nor can time be made up of 'nows.' In *Physics* 241a, it is stated,

> οὔτε γὰρ ὁ χρόνος ἐκ τῶν νῦν οὔθ' ἡ γραμμὴ ἐκ στιγμῶν οὔθ' ἡ κίνησις ἐκ κινημάτων· οὐθὲν γὰρ ἄλλο ποιεῖ ὁ τοῦτο λέγων ἢ τὴν κίνησιν ἐξ ἀμερῶν, καθάπερ ἂν εἰ τὸν χρόνον ἐκ τῶν νῦν ἢ τὸ μῆκος ἐκ στιγμῶν.[37]

> For neither does time consist of 'nows,' nor a line of points, nor motion of motions [κινημάτων]. For the one saying this makes nothing other than motion of non-parts, just as if [he] would [make] time consist of 'nows' or a length of points.

Instead, τὸ δὲ μεταξὺ τῶν νῦν χρόνος 'that which is *between* the 'nows' is time'[38] (my italics). Here Goldschmidt errs when he refers to time that passes between two 'nows' as a second sense of the term 'now,' unless he refers to Aristotle's discussion of the *cognitively* perceived notion of an extended 'now.'[39]

Tying things together we should take note of Aristotle's comment in *Physics* 251b on the function of the 'now' in relation to the existence of time, "Therefore, if it is impossible for time both to exist, and to perceive [it] without the 'now,' . . ." Here, on his way to making another point,

---

[34] G. E. L. Owen, "Aristotle on Time," in *Motion and Time, Space and Matter: Interrelations in the History of Philosophy and Science,* ed. Peter Machamer and Robert Turnbull, (Columbus: Ohio State University Press, 1976), 296–301.

[35] Coope, *Time for Aristotle: Physics IV.10–14,* 26.

[36] Aristotle, *Physica,* 234a31.

[37] Ibid., 241a2–6.

[38] Ibid., 237a10–11.

[39] Goldschmidt, *Temps physique et temps tragique chez Aristote: Commentaire sur le Quatrième livre de la Physique (10–14) et sur la Poétique,* 153.

Aristotle assumes the existence of time on the basis of the 'now.'[40] Time thus has actual existence in the 'now.'

That the 'now' has an essential role to play for the existence of time is an issue we now turn to.

6.3 In Context: Time as Infinite Past and Future or Eternal 'Now'

In Sect. 5.3 we noted the aporetic contrast between locating existing time either in an eternal 'now' or in past and future time, but both alternatives were rejected on the grounds that the 'now' is merely a boundary and that neither past nor future time exists. In the contrast between time from the broadest possible perspective, that of infinite extension into past and future, and its narrowest, that of having its point of departure in the extension-less present 'now,' it seems they are prerequisites for one another. For in *Physics* 251b, picking up where we ended in previous section, we note that when discussing whether time has at some point come into existence or whether time has always existed, Aristotle discusses the contrast between the 'now' as a limit of past and future time.

> εἰ οὖν ἀδύνατόν ἐστιν καὶ εἶναι καὶ νοῆσαι χρόνον ἄνευ τοῦ νῦν, τὸ δὲ νῦν ἐστι μεσότης τις, καὶ ἀρχὴν καὶ τελευτὴν ἔχον ἅμα, ἀρχὴν μὲν τοῦ ἐσομένου χρόνου, τελευτὴν δὲ τοῦ παρελθόντος, ἀνάγκη ἀεὶ εἶναι χρόνον. τὸ γὰρ ἔσχατον τοῦ τελευταίου ληφθέντος χρόνου ἔν τινι τῶν νῦν ἔσται (οὐδὲν γὰρ ἔστι λαβεῖν ἐν τῷ χρόνῳ παρὰ τὸ νῦν), ὥστ' ἐπεί ἐστιν ἀρχή τε καὶ τελευτὴ τὸ νῦν, ἀνάγκη αὐτοῦ ἐπ' ἀμφότερα εἶναι ἀεὶ χρόνον.[41]

Therefore, if it is impossible for time both to exist, and to perceive [it] without the 'now,' and [if] the 'now' is some mediator [μεσότης], having both the beginning and the end at the same time, on the one hand a beginning of the time that will be and, on the other, an end of what passed, it is necessary for time always to exist. For the last of the uttermost time that is perceived will be in some one of the 'nows' (for there is nothing to perceive [λαβεῖν] in time except[42] the 'now'), and so, since the 'now' is both a beginning and an end, it is necessary that time is always on both [sides] of it.

---

[40] Aristotle, *Physica*, 251b19–20; cf. Boudreault, "Aristotle's Account of Time: A Moderate Realism", 206. Inwood correctly notes that the occurrence of the 'now' is sufficient "to secure the existence of time" (Inwood, "Aristotle on the Reality of Time", 177).

[41] Aristotle, *Physica*, 251b19–26.

[42] Or 'apart from.'

To begin with we should note, again, that Aristotle *assumes* the *existence* of time, "if it is impossible for time both to exist, and to perceive [it] without the 'now,' . . .' " Further, Aristotle poses a symbiotic relationship between the 'now' and time. It is by the function of the 'now' that past and future time can be said to *exist*, since the 'now' serves as a limit between the two.[43] Goldschmidt similarly comments, "L'instant est au centre de l'analyse aristotélicienne du temps ... c'est la distinction des instants qui permet de percevoir l'existence du temps [The moment is at the centre of the Aristotelian analysis of time ... it is the distinction between moments that allows the perception of the existence of time]."[44] Even in relation to the distant past, Aristotle notes, "For the last of the uttermost time that is perceived will be in some one of the 'nows' (for there is nothing to perceive [λαβεῖν] in time except[45] the 'now')."[46] Harry goes too far when she argues that the *Physics* is not the place for Aristotle to discuss infinite time and posits too strong a contrast between infinite time and time as an essential feature of motion;[47] it would rather seem that infinite time is a prerequisite and basis for the more focused study of time around that breaking point, the 'now,' between past and future that we find in *Physics* IV.10–14. At the very end of our passage Aristotle asserts that an effect of the fact that the 'now' constitutes the end of the past and the beginning of the future, time, as a necessity, is consistently on both sides of the 'now,' "since the 'now' is both a beginning and an end, it is necessary that time is always on both [sides] of it."

In *Physics* 219b–220a, the interdependence between the 'now' and time is brought out even more clearly,

---

[43] Roark also notes that "were there no now, there could be no time." (Roark, *Aristotle on Time: A Study of Physics*, 213).

[44] Goldschmidt, *Temps physique et temps tragique chez Aristote: Commentaire sur le Quatrième livre de la Physique (10–14) et sur la Poétique*, 147; my translation.

[45] Or 'apart from.'

[46] For the centrality of the 'now' for the perception of time, see Sarah Waterlow (Sarah Waterlow, "Aristotle's Now," *The Philosophical Quarterly (1950-)* 34, no. 135 (1984):, 127); Thomas Seissl asks why Aristotle does not define time relative to the 'now' if indeed it is so central; instead, he notes, time is defined as a number in regard to the 'before' and 'after' (Seissl, "Aristotle's "Now" and the Definition of Time: Method and Exegesis in Simplicius' Interpretation of Physics IV. 10", 367). The answer is that the 'before' and 'after' is the before and after of the 'now,' which means that the 'now' indeed is at the centre.

[47] Harry, *Chronos in Aristotle's Physics: On the Nature of Time*, 37.

εἴτε χρόνος μὴ εἴη, τὸ νῦν οὐκ ἂν εἴη, εἴτε τὸ νῦν μὴ εἴη, χρόνος οὐκ ἂν εἴη· ἅμα γὰρ ὥσπερ τὸ φερόμενον καὶ ἡ φορά, . . . καὶ συνεχής τε δὴ ὁ χρόνος τῷ νῦν, καὶ διῄρηται κατὰ τὸ νῦν.[48]

Neither would there be any time if there were no 'now,' nor would there be any 'now' if there were no time. For they are together, just as the moving thing [τὸ φερόμενον] and motion [ἡ φορά], . . . And time, then, is both continuous by the 'now,' and divided according to the 'now.'

Again, Aristotle assumes the existence of time, "Neither would there be time . . ." Aristotle argues that there is a mutual interdependence between time and the 'now' where neither would exist without the other, "Neither would there be any time if there were no 'now,' nor would there be any 'now' if there were no time." They are as necessary to one another as the moving thing and motion are to one another. The 'now' is both the basis for time's continuity and its constant (potential) dividing between past and future, "And time, then, is both continuous by the 'now,' and divided according to the 'now.' "[49]

We conclude that the 'now' and time—past, future and infinite time—are prerequisites for one another, since neither would exist without the other, and that time is located in, and constituted by, the 'now' in combination with preceding and following time.

6.4 In Context: Time as a Cognitive-Perceptive or a Mathematical-Logical Category

As noted in Sect. 5.4, it seems Aristotle, on the one hand, approaches time as a matter of strict, mathematical and logical necessity, and, on the other, as a category dependent on subjective consciousness and cognition. Discussing Joachim's observation of the conception of the 'now' as an abstract mathematical limit without content, on the one hand, and as an experienced present that is a whole with a content, on the other,[50] Goldschmidt argues that there are "deux conceptions réellement différentes [two clearly different understandings]."[51] Further down he states,

---

[48] Aristotle, *Physica*, 219b33–220a2, 220a4–5.
[49] Kretzmann comments that the 'now' is quantitively stable (Kretzmann, "Time Exists-but Hardly, or Obscurely", 97).
[50] Aristotle, *Aristotle: The Nicomachean Ethics; a commentary by H. H. Joachim*, 278–279.
[51] Goldschmidt, *Temps physique et temps tragique chez Aristote: Commentaire sur le Quatrième livre de la Physique (10–14) et sur la Poétique*, 148; my translation.

Il parait donc préférable d'accepter, comme tel, le double emploi du mot instant et, plutôt que d'y avoir une contradiction ou une confusion, de l'expliquer par la différence des deux discipline où il a lieux.

It therefore seems preferable to accept, as such, a double use of the word 'now' and, rather than that there being a contradiction or confusion, to explain it by the difference between the two disciplines in which it occurs.[52]

In other words, as we will argue below, the 'now' may either be perceived in terms of mathematics and physics as a strict limit, or as a psychological entity—a perceived, or experienced, 'now.' Ruggiu argues along similar lines in favour of a holistic approach that takes into account the phenomenological experience of time,

> Un tale tipo di analisi richiede che non si distingua tra interno ed esterno, tra temporalità che affetta le cose della natura e esperienza interiore della temporalità.
>
> Such a kind of analysis requires that we do not distinguish between internal and external, between temporality that affects the things of nature and the internal experience of temporality.[53]

Ruggiu points to the necessity of bringing together the external expression of time and the internal experience of time as a phenomenon.

As we follow Aristotle's continued discussion of these two viewpoints, where the former perhaps could be said to dominate, we note that he, however, multiple times returns to the role of consciousness and perception in relation to time.

As early as in *Physics* 189a Aristotle discusses two methodological approaches for the study of nature, which also apply to time, being one of the major categories of study,[54]

> καὶ οἱ μὲν γνωριμώτερα κατὰ τὸν λόγον, . . . οἱ δὲ κατὰ τὴν αἴσθησιν (τὸ μὲν γὰρ καθόλου κατὰ τὸν λόγον γνώριμον, τὸ δὲ καθ' ἕκαστον κατὰ τὴν αἴσθησιν· ὁ μὲν γὰρ λόγος τοῦ καθόλου, ἡ δ' αἴσθησις τοῦ κατὰ μέρος).[55]

---

[52] Ibid., 149; my translation.
[53] Ruggiu, *Aristotele: Fisica; saggio introduttivo, traduzione, note e apparati*, XLVII; my translation.
[54] *Physics* 202b: "The study of Nature is concerned with extension, motion, and time." (Aristotle, *Physics*, 215).
[55] Aristotle, *Physica*, 189a4–8.

6 RESOLVING THE APORETIC CONTRASTS IN CONTEXT 59

And some things are more intelligible according to reason [τὸν λόγον], ... other things according to perception [αἴσθησιν] (for the whole,[56] on the one hand, is known according to reason, but the particular [τὸ ... καθ' ἕκαστον], on the other, according to perception. For reason, on the one hand, is in regard[57] to the whole, but perception, on the other, in regard to the part).

Here Aristotle accounts for a rough division between a rational and an empirical approach that can be applied to the concept of time, a division between what can be concluded in regard to the nature of time on mathematical and logical grounds and what can be noticed about its characteristics on the basis of observation, that is, both in terms of physical perception and how this visual perception is cognitively conceptualised. Both of these approaches can be noted in Aristotle's chapters on time. However, in his three ἀπορίαι we mostly find mathematical-logical reasoning with only some slight references to the cognitive-perceptual elements in the discussion of time. Therefore, we will here take note of more references to this approach to Aristotle's understanding of time. Terms that occur with some frequency in Aristotle's five chapters on time describing time include 'think,' 'conscious/ness,' 'perception'/'perceive', 'notice,' 'seem,' 'impression,' 'appear,' 'distinguish,' 'mark out' and 'mind.'

In *Physics* 218b, Aristotle states,

ὅταν γὰρ μηδὲν αὐτοὶ μεταβάλλωμεν τὴν διάνοιαν ἢ λάθωμεν μεταβάλλοντες, οὐ δοκεῖ ἡμῖν γεγονέναι χρόνος[58]

For whenever we ourselves do not change at all with regard to the *mind* or we change not *noticing* it, it does not *seem* to us that [any] time has passed.[59]

Here he points to consciousness, or lack thereof, in regard to the correlation between change and time. If change is not experienced or even if it is that we for some reason do not pay attention to it, we have no awareness of any passage of time. A few lines down, as Aristotle elaborates, using the fable of the men who were asleep with the heroes in Sardinia, he notes

---

[56] Or 'the general'; however, it seems 'the whole' fits better here because in the next sentence "τοῦ καθόλου" is contrasted with "μέρος" 'part.'
[57] *Or* 'is of.'
[58] Ibid., 218b21–23.
[59] My italics.

that when time has passed between two 'nows,' they are, "because of the lack of *perception*,"[60] fused into one and the same 'now.' Further down he states,

εἰ δὴ τὸ μὴ οἴεσθαι εἶναι χρόνον τότε συμβαίνει ἡμῖν, ὅταν μὴ ὁρίσωμεν μηδεμίαν μεταβολήν, ἀλλ᾽ ἐν ἑνὶ καὶ ἀδιαιρέτῳ φαίνηται ἡ ψυχὴ μένειν, ὅταν δ᾽ αἰσθώμεθα καὶ ὁρίσωμεν, τότε φαμὲν γεγονέναι χρόνον[61]

If then we do not *think* there is any time, then it happens to us whenever we do not mark out any change, but the *mind* appears to remain in the one and undivided [state], but whenever we *perceive* and *mark out boundaries*, then we declare time to have passed.[62]

To Aristotle the awareness of time (through the perception of change) is not limited to what is visually perceived, but it may be enough with 'imagined' perception within the mind (219a),

καὶ γὰρ ἐὰν ᾖ σκότος καὶ μηδὲν διὰ τοῦ σώματος πάσχωμεν, κίνησις δέ τις ἐν τῇ ψυχῇ ἐνῇ, εὐθὺς ἅμα δοκεῖ τις γεγονέναι καὶ χρόνος. ἀλλὰ μὴν καὶ ὅταν γε χρόνος δοκῇ γεγονέναι τις, ἅμα καὶ κίνησίς τις δοκεῖ γεγονέναι[63]

For even if there would be darkness and we would *receive no impression* through the body, but there would be some movement in the *mind*, straightway it *seems* at once that some time has also passed. But on the other hand, also whenever time would *seem* to have passed, at once also some movement *seems* to have passed.[64]

Aristotle's description corresponds to what has been noted in neuroscience, that on-line perceptual experience stored in memory may be made use of in off-line processing and cognitive conceptualisation, i.e. cognitively conceptualised time capitalises on prior perceptions of time.[65] Mark Turner calls this "mental simulation."[66] Aristotle's example is not so far-

---

[60] Ibid., 218b26: διὰ τὴν ἀναισθησίαν; my italics.
[61] Ibid., 218b29–32.
[62] My italics; cf. Torres, "La aporética del tiempo: Un análisis reconstructivo de Fis. Δ 10, 217b29–218b20", 217.
[63] Aristotle, *Physica*, 219a4–8.
[64] My italics.
[65] Evans and Green, *Cognitive Linguistics: An Introduction*, 240–242.
[66] Mark Turner, "Opening Commentary: Polytropos and Communication in the Wild," in *The Cambridge Handbook of Cognitive Linguistics*, ed. Barbara Dancygier, (Cambridge: Cambridge University Press, 2017), 93.

fetched from the viewpoint of modern experience. Imagine sitting alone in an empty waiting room with no clock on the wall, where there is no movement around you and nothing happens, or, closer to Aristotle's example, lying awake in your bed at night not being able to fall asleep; intuitively it may feel like the time is standing still. Yet, the passing of time may be conceptualised on the basis of prior experience. On the other hand, if there is much movement around you or you are on journey, the experience of the passing of time is more explicit. Such claims find support in the work of Michael Flaherty who argues that in the first case circumstances of monotony are perceived as temporally slow, whereas in the second case circumstances that are full of intense impressions may be perceived as having longer temporal duration than they in fact have.[67] Vyvyan Evans and Melanie Green underestimate the significance of external perception when they argue that the experience of the domain of time has a more intrinsic basis.[68]

Further down in *Physics* 219a–b, Aristotle talks about a 'now' being *perceived*[69] and how we speak about time "But whenever [we perceive] a 'before' and 'after,' then we say there is time."[70] Without here going into the many exciting implications of these statements in *Physics* 218b–219b, we simply note the abundant presence of cognitive-perceptual language. One of the most striking claims of Aristotle (in *Physics* 223a25–28) is that time does not exist without the corroboration of a perceiving mind, except in a very restricted sense. Michael Bruder likewise notes the dependence of time on the perception of the mind.[71]

Finally, in *Physics* 223a, Aristotle explicitly notes the worthy task of investigating the correlation between time and conscience, "But it is also worthy of investigation how, at any time, time relates to *consciousness*."[72] This may be one of the first references to the early beginning of cognitive

---

[67] Michael G. Flaherty, *A Watched Pot: How We Experience Time* (New York: New York University Press, 1999), 52, 60.

[68] Evans and Green, *Cognitive Linguistics: An Introduction*, 235.

[69] Aristotle, *Physica*, 219a30–31: ὅταν μὲν οὖν ὡς ἓν τὸ νῦν αἰσθανώμεθα 'Thus, whenever we on the one hand perceive the 'now' as one'; my italics.

[70] Ibid., 219a31–b1: ὅταν δὲ τὸ πρότερον καὶ ὕστερον, τότε λέγομεν χρόνον·; my italics.

[71] Bruder, "The Time of Our Lives: Aristotle on Time, Temporal Perception, Recollection, and Habituation.", 44.

[72] Aristotle, *Physica*, 223a16–17: ἄξιον δ' ἐπισκέψεως καὶ πῶς ποτε ἔχει ὁ χρόνος πρὸς τὴν ψυχήν; my italics.

science. It is noteworthy that Aristotle in *On interpretation*[73] argues that "the perceptions of the mind are the same for all men." This points to the shared neuroanatomical and cognitive architecture of all humans and their shared experience of the world as selfs relative to the surrounding world in regard to the experience of time, whether sensory experience or introspective experience.[74] It is noteworthy that so many of the elements in Aristotle's theory on time correspond to the very small set of words and concepts (around 65) that are shared by almost all language users of the world, as noted in the cognitive linguistic model Natural Semantic Metalanguage, such as *I, think, know, before, after, now, when, moment, short time, long time, move* and *happen*.[75] These words and concepts relate to what is subjective or experiential by way of perception, and to the human body, and may constitute contrastive pairs.[76] These observations point to a fairly universal understanding of time as noted by Aristotle.

We conclude that the data clearly suggest that Aristotle in his investigation of the concept of time strives for a combination of mathematical-logical thought, on the one hand, and empirical observations on how humans perceive, whether physically or cognitively, and interpret time and its passage, on the other. To Aristotle, there is no irreconcilable contrast between these two approaches in his discussion on time.

6.5 In Context: Time as Partaker of Substance or Not

The question of time's partaking of substance is divided into two questions, one of which has been resolved, *viz.* that of time's existence that we dealt with in Sect. 6.2, where we concluded that time has existence either actually or potentially. We also noted that Aristotle in general terms assumes the existence of time, that time exists on both sides of the 'now.' With this solution part of the problem of whether time partakes of

---

[73] Aristotle, *De interpretatione*, ed. L. Minio-Paluello, 16a5–8; ταὐτὰ πᾶσι παθήματα τῆς ψυχῆς.

[74] Evans and Green, *Cognitive Linguistics: An Introduction*, 55, 63–67; Ungerer and Schmid, *An Introduction to Cognitive Linguistics*, 32–33; Talmy Givón, *On Understanding Grammar* (New York: Academic Press, 1979), 129.

[75] Cliff Goddard, "Natural Semantic Metalanguage," in *The Routledge Handbook of Cognitive Linguistics*, ed. Xu Wen and John R. Taylor, (New York: Routledge, 2021), 93–94.

[76] Ibid., 95; in regard to the subjective experience of time, see Jan H. Nylund, "The Potential of Linguistic Theories in the Study of Aspect and Tense in Ancient Greek, With Particular Attention to New Testament Greek" (Ph.D. thesis, Lund University, 2024), 271.

substance is solved. But the second question is how something that does not have a physical existence may be said to partake of substance. Ruggiu is too quick to dismiss οὐσία 'substance,' which, as noted, he does not even bother to translate in the first ἀπορία, as an element of what makes up Aristotle's understanding of time, when he denotes a solution that depends on οὐσία as a "concezione volgare [popular conception]."[77] As for the importance of οὐσία 'substance' in Aristotle's understanding of time Gernot Böhme correctly argues that "Wenn sie [Zeit] nicht selbst οὐσία (Substanz) ist, so muß sie irgendwie an der Substanz vorliegen [If it [time] not itself is οὐσία (substance), it must somehow be present in the substance."[78] Walter Mesch notes the significance of the fact that Aristotle's discussion on time is found in *Physics*, "Die aristotelische Zeittheorie gehört damit primär in eine naturphilosophische Untersuchung der Bewegung (kinêsis) [The Aristotelian time theory belongs therefore primarily to a nature-philosophical enquiry into motion (kinêsis)]."[79]

On the matter of the place of substance in Aristotle's conception of time we find an enlightening text passage in *Physics* 190a, where Aristotle states,

ἁπλῶς δὲ γίγνεσθαι τῶν οὐσιῶν μόνον, κατὰ μὲν τἆλλα φανερὸν ὅτι ἀνάγκη ὑποκεῖσθαί τι τὸ γιγνόμενον (καὶ γὰρ ποσὸν καὶ ποιὸν καὶ πρὸς ἕτερον [καὶ ποτὲ] καὶ ποῦ γίγνεται ὑποκειμένου τινὸς διὰ τὸ μόνην τὴν οὐσίαν μηθενὸς κατ' ἄλλου λέγεσθαι ὑποκειμένου, τὰ δ' ἄλλα πάντα κατὰ τῆς οὐσίας).[80]

But to come into being [γίγνεσθαι] in the absolute sense[81] [ἁπλῶς] is, on the one hand, only [said] of substances [οὐσιῶν], but on the other, in regard to all other things it is evident that it is necessary that something underlies [ὑποκεῖσθαί] that which comes to pass (for not only [καὶ] quantity [ποσὸν] but also [καὶ] quality [ποιὸν] and [a relation] to another [πρὸς ἕτερον] [thing] [and time [ποτὲ]] and place [ποῦ] arise from something underlying [ὑποκειμένου τινὸς], because substance [οὐσίαν] alone is spoken of in terms of no other underlying thing [ὑποκειμένου], but all the others [are spoken of] in terms of the substance [τῆς οὐσίας].

[77] Ruggiu, *Aristotele: Fisica; saggio introduttivo, traduzione, note e apparati*, XLVI; my translation.
[78] Gernot Böhme, *Zeit und Zahl. Studien zur Zeittheorie bei Platon, Aristoteles, Leibniz und Kant* (Frankfurt a. M.: V. Klostermann, 1974), 162.
[79] Mesch, "Zeit", 463; my translation.
[80] Aristotle, *Physica*, 190a32–190b1.
[81] *LSJ* ἁπλ-ῶς, II.2.

From this passage it is implied (and corroborated in Aristotle's metaphysics) that things such as quantity, quality and time, have 'being' without in themselves being substances. Instead, they are characteristics, or affections, *of* substances. For instance, each substance has a quantity and a number of qualities. While it is not difficult to grasp the fact that a substance such as an apple has a quantity and qualities that change and develop as it grows, it is not quite that easy to get a hold of what the underlying thing of time is, but obviously time has an underlying thing (τὸ ὑποκείμενον) according to Aristotle, "but on the other, in regard to all other things it is evident that it is necessary that something underlies [ὑποκεῖσθαί] that which comes to pass." This text not only corroborates that time has an underlying thing (τὸ ὑποκείμενον), but also that these "other things" have a direct relation to something underlying in which they, so to speak, partake. In other words, time too partakes in substance by its connection to its underlying thing. The question is what τὸ ὑποκείμενον 'the underlying thing' of time is.

As noted in *Physics* 220b, time is dependent on motion as motion is dependent on magnitude,

> ὁμοίως δὲ καὶ ἐπὶ τοῦ χρόνου καὶ τῆς κινήσεως· τῷ μὲν γὰρ χρόνῳ τὴν κίνησιν, τῇ δὲ κινήσει τὸν χρόνον μετροῦμεν. καὶ τοῦτ' εὐλόγως συμβέβηκεν· ἀκολουθεῖ γὰρ τῷ μὲν μεγέθει ἡ κίνησις, τῇ δὲ κινήσει ὁ χρόνος, τῷ καὶ ποσὰ καὶ συνεχῆ καὶ διαιρετὰ εἶναι· διὰ μὲν γὰρ τὸ τὸ μέγεθος εἶναι τοιοῦτον ἡ κίνησις ταῦτα πέπονθεν, διὰ δὲ τὴν κίνησιν ὁ χρόνος.[82]

> But likewise both in regard to time and to motion. For, on the one hand, by time [χρόνῳ] we measure motion [κίνησιν] but, on the other, by motion time. And in this way it has with good reason turned out [συμβέβηκεν]: For motion, on the one hand, follows magnitude [μεγέθει], and time, on the other, follows motion; by the being [τῷ . . . εἶναι] not only in regard to quantity [ποσὰ] but also continuity [συνεχῆ] and divisions [διαιρετὰ]. For, on the one hand, because magnitude [μέγεθος] is such as this [τοιοῦτον], motion has come to be in a state [πέπονθεν] in regard to these [magnitudes], and time because of motion.

On some basic level Aristotle notes the mutual dependence of time and motion, as they measure one another, "For, on the one hand, by time [χρόνῳ] we measure motion [κίνησιν] but, on the other, by motion time." However, as Aristotle elaborates, it is evident that there is an order of

---

[82] Ibid., 220b22–28.

dependence, "For motion, on the one hand, follows magnitude [μεγέθει], and time, on the other, follows motion; by the being [τῷ . . . εἶναι] not only in regard to quantity [ποσὰ] but also continuity [συνεχῆ] and divisions [διαιρετὰ]." This dependence can schematically be expressed as follows: magnitude > motion > time, where motion depends on magnitude and time depends on motion.[83] Aristotle offers more detail towards this understanding in the final clause, "For, on the one hand, because magnitude [μέγεθος] is such as this [τοιοῦτον], motion has come to be in a state [πέπονθεν] in regard to these [magnitudes], and time because of motion."[84] Here Aristotle's observation of multiple *image schemas*, that is, *holistic sensory-perceptual experiences*, which originate from his pre-conceptual experience of interaction with the world around him, are extended to the more abstract concept of time. Image schemas, as for example *bounded space*, *container*, *path* and *locomotion* serve as a basis for evolving a *conceptual projection* where embodied notions are extended to the notion of time.[85] Within a bounded space or container (magnitude >) there is locomotion along a path (motion >) which is conceptualised into the notion of time (> time). Todd Oakley notes that an image schema "is a condensed redescription of perceptual experience for the purpose of mapping spatial structure onto conceptual structure."[86] Aristotle translates his perceptual experience of motion in space into a conceptual time structure. It is noteworthy that it more lately, in the 1970s onwards, has been argued, quite in

---

[83] Cf. Bostock who notes the ontological dependence of time on motion and of motion on substance (David Bostock, "Aristotle's Account of Time," *Phronesis* 25, no. 2 (1980):, 165).

[84] On this point, see also Aristotle, *Physics*, 259, 261: "Illimitability does not stand for the same thing in magnitude, movement and time, but differs in accordance with their several natures in a determined order of priority. For continuity, in which the unlimited potentialities inhere, has a stable existence in magnitude, but movement (including modification and growth) is continuous because the magnitude over which it focuses is so, and time is so because it is the comparative register of movement."

[85] On image schemas and embodiment, see Evans and Green, *Cognitive Linguistics: An Introduction*, 46, 158, 183–84; Dirk Geeraerts, "Cognitive Semantics," in *The Routledge Handbook of Cognitive Linguistics*, ed. Xu Wen and John R. Taylor, (New York: Routledge, 2021), 22; Xu Wen and Canzhong Jiang, "Embodiment," in *The Routledge Handbook of Cognitive Linguistics*, ed. Xu Wen and John R. Taylor, (New York: Routledge, 2021), 148; Jan H. Nylund, "The Potential of Linguistic Theories in the Study of Aspect and Tense in Ancient Greek, With Particular Attention to New Testament Greek", 275–77.

[86] Todd Oakley, "Image Schemas," in *The Oxford Handbook of Cognitive Linguistics*, ed. Dirk Geeraerts and Hubert Cuyckens, (Oxford: Oxford University Press, 2007), 215; on image schemas, see also Dennis Tay, "Image Schemas," in *The Routledge Handbook of Cognitive Linguistics*, ed. Xu Wen and John R. Taylor, (New York: Routledge, 2021).

agreement with Aristotle's understanding, that the way we talk about time depends on the notion of motion in a three-dimensional space.[87]

In this hierarchy motion underlies time.[88] The close correlation between time and motion is also implied in two texts in *Physics* 223a and *Physics* 251b,

ἢ ὅτι κινήσεώς τι πάθος ἢ ἕξις, ἀριθμός γε ὤν, . . . ὁ δὲ χρόνος καὶ ἡ κίνησις ἅμα κατά τε δύναμιν καὶ κατ' ἐνέργειαν;[89]

. . . or because [time] is some property [πάθος] or permanent condition [ἕξις] of motion, since [time] at any rate is a number |[of motion]][90], . . . But time and motion are together both according to potentiality [δύναμιν] and actuality [ἐνέργειαν].

ἀλλὰ μὴν εἴ γε χρόνον, φανερὸν ὅτι ἀνάγκη εἶναι καὶ κίνησιν, εἴπερ ὁ χρόνος πάθος τι κινήσεως.[91]

But if time at any rate [is], it is evident that it is a necessity that motion too is, since time is some property of motion.

In *Physics* 223a, Aristotle identifies time as a quality of motion—or as Inwood puts it, "a derivative phenomenon"[92]—"because [time] is some property [πάθος] or permanent condition [ἕξις] of motion." Aristotle underlines the close correlation between time and motion, where time functions as a measurer of motion, "since [time] at any rate is a number |[of motion]]."[93] Time thus measures and numerates the underlying

---

[87] Vyvyan Evans, *The Structure of Time: Language, Meaning and Temporal Cognition* (Amsterdam/Philadelphia: John Benjamins Publishing Company, 2003), 13; see also others, such as Elizabeth Closs Traugott, "Spatial Expressions of Tense and Temporal Sequencing," *Semiotica* 15, no. 3 (1975): 207–230; Suzanne Fleischman, "The Past and the Future," *Berkeley Linguistics Society* 8, (1983): 322–334; Frank Brisard, "A Critique of Localism in and About Tense Theory" (Ph.D. thesis, University of Antwerp, 1999), and Leonard Talmy, *Toward a Cognitive Semantics, 2 Volumes* (Cambridge, Mass.: MIT press, 2000).

[88] Harry, in general terms, tentatively argues in this direction, "it will not be a surprise if time [. . .] in Aristotle's analytic of time turns out to be not a being *qua* itself but an attribute of motion." (Harry, *Chronos in Aristotle's Physics: On the Nature of Time*, 33); further ahead Harry states that time is "a term of *kinēsis*" (Ibid., 37).

[89] Aristotle, *Physica*, 223a18–21.

[90] Added as a clarification though not implied in the immediate context, but elsewhere in Aristotle's text on time it is clearly indicated that time is 'a number of motion.'

[91] Ibid., 251b26–27.

[92] Inwood, "Aristotle on the Reality of Time", 153.

[93] Roark correctly argues that "time owes its existence immediately to motion and perception, and ultimately to material objects, substances" (Roark, *Aristotle on Time: A Study of Physics*, 3).

motion.⁹⁴ This is corroborated in *Physics* 251b, where Aristotle asserts that time is a quality of motion, "since time is some property of motion." That is, time qualifies the underlying thing, motion, or more specifically, the moving thing (whatever it is). The belongingness of time and motion in relation to one another is asserted in the last line of the text from *Physics* 223a, "But time and motion are together both according to potentiality [δύναμιν] and actuality [ἐνέργειαν]."⁹⁵ Wherever there is motion, whether potential or actual, time is there measuring it. In cosmic time which is based on cosmic motion, the motion of celestial bodies, such as the sun, a precise correlation is established between motion in space and time; Michel Ghins asserts that "equal space intervals are travelled in equal times."⁹⁶ This means that McGinnis criticism on this point is unwarranted.⁹⁷

Inwood, noting the analogy between the moving object and the 'now,' questions why we need to "suppose that there is some persistent temporal entity which underlies or consists of the successive 'nows' in the way that the persisting object underlies or consists of its successive states."⁹⁸ The reason for his doubt is his claim that the object in itself is considerably different compared to the 'now' in that it could remain the same without moving or changing, or it could be an object "qua moving."⁹⁹ Inwood thinks Aristotle is neglectful in failing to take into account this distinction. However, here we have to consider the fact that Aristotle all through his enquiry into the nature of time and the 'now' conducts his enquiry close up to his object of study, focusing on the 'now' as the intersection between past and future time, only to zoom out towards the end of his enquiry, in *Physics* IV.14,¹⁰⁰ where he discusses the nature of time from a macro-perspective. It will here suffice to cite a key passage,

⁹⁴ In this discussion of the 'now,' it is clear that Roark (along the same lines as motion underlies time) argues that "a kinetic cut," i.e. a slice of motion, underlies the 'now.' Roark: "a kinetic cut is the material constituent of a now." (Ibid., 215).
⁹⁵ The connection between time and motion is thus much stronger than a mere analogy as suggested by Julia Annas (Julia Annas, "Aristotle, Number and Time," *The Philosophical Quarterly (1950-)* 25, no. 99 (1975): 97–113, 110). Cf. Alfred Dunshirn, "Das ‚Jetzt 'in Aristoteles' Zeittheorie: Zu Physik IV 11, 219 b 10–25," *Wiener Studien* Band 119/2006, (2006): 63–75, 67.
⁹⁶ Michel Ghins, "Two Difficulties with Regard to Aristotle's Treatment of Time," *Revue de Philosophie Ancienne* 9, no. 1 (1991):, 85.
⁹⁷ McGinnis, "Making Time Aristotle's Way", 157.
⁹⁸ Inwood, "Aristotle on the Reality of Time", 165.
⁹⁹ Ibid., 165–166.
¹⁰⁰ Aristotle, *Physica*, 223b21–224a2.

διὸ καὶ δοκεῖ ὁ χρόνος εἶναι ἡ τῆς σφαίρας κίνησις, ὅτι ταύτῃ μετροῦνται αἱ ἄλλαι κινήσεις καὶ ὁ χρόνος ταύτῃ τῇ κινήσει.[101]

Therefore it also seems time is the motion of the sphere [τῆς σφαίρας], because by this all other motions are measured and by this motion time [is measured].

As implied here, it is the "motion of the sphere," or more precisely put for our purposes, the motion of the heavenly bodies, primarily the rotation of the sun and the moon that is the benchmark for the measurement both of other motions and of time. This means that when Aristotle's micro enquiry into time is placed into its macro-context, Inwood's worry about non-moving objects goes way;[102] left is *the* object *qua* moving, the sun, whose rotation is constant. The sun, primarily, is the underlying constantly moving substance of time, and specifically the 'now.'[103]

We conclude that time indeed is a partaker of substance by being a quality of the motion of a moving thing, a *substance*, and that motion functions as τὸ ὑποκείμενον 'the underlying thing' of time.

6.6 In Context: 'Nows' as the Parts of Time or Not

In regard to the question whether 'nows' are parts of time or not, we note within the triple ἀπορία a tension between the tentative statement "time [χρόνος] does not *seem* to be composed of 'nows [νῦν]'"[104] and the reference to 'nows' as "one part [μέρος] after another," on the one hand, and the final argument in the third ἀπορία, where the 'now' is not a part of time, on the other.

In *Physics* 239b, Aristotle explicitly asserts,

---

[101] Ibid., 223b21–23.

[102] Bostock seems to have the same worry, pointing to the potential rest of an object and therefore claiming that Aristotle's argument to connect time and motion fails; however, with the cosmic motion that Aristotle has in mind there is no potential rest (Bostock, "Aristotle's Account of Time", 166).

[103] Claudiu Mesaroş also points to time's connection to circular motion (Claudiu Mesaroş, "Aristotle on Becoming and Meanings of Time," in *The Time is Now. Essays on the Philosophy of Becoming,* ed. Mihaela Gligor, (Bucharest: Zeta Books, 2020), 106).

[104] My italics.

6 RESOLVING THE APORETIC CONTRASTS IN CONTEXT 69

οὐ γὰρ σύγκειται ὁ χρόνος ἐκ τῶν νῦν τῶν ἀδιαιρέτων, ὥσπερ οὐδ' ἄλλο μέγεθος οὐδέν.[105]

For time [χρόνος] is not composed of indivisible 'nows,' just as magnitude [μέγεθος] is not [composed] of anything other.

Here Aristotle clearly states that time, in analogy with magnitude, is not composed of 'nows.'

A prerequisite for the 'now' to indeed be *a* part of time is that the 'now' has extension. In a discussion in *Physics* 234a, on the possibility of the point indicating the end of the past and the point indicating the beginning of the future not being the same, Aristotle posits hypothetically that the 'now' would itself then be a period of time, and therefore have extension, "the 'now' [would be] divisible."[106]

Aristotle comments further (234a),

εἰ δὲ διαιρετὸν τὸ νῦν, ἔσται τι τοῦ γεγονότος ἐν τῷ μέλλοντι καὶ τοῦ μέλλοντος ἐν τῷ γεγονότι· καθ' ὃ γὰρ ἂν διαιρεθῇ, τοῦτο διοριεῖ τὸν παρήκοντα καὶ τὸν μέλλοντα χρόνον. ἅμα δὲ καὶ οὐκ ἂν καθ' αὑτὸ εἴη τὸ νῦν, ἀλλὰ καθ' ἕτερον· ἡ γὰρ διαίρεσις οὐ καθ' αὑτό. πρὸς δὲ τούτοις τοῦ νῦν τὸ μέν τι γεγονὸς ἔσται τὸ δὲ μέλλον, καὶ οὐκ ἀεὶ τὸ αὐτὸ γεγονὸς ἢ μέλλον. οὐδὲ δὴ τὸ νῦν τὸ αὐτό· πολλαχῇ γὰρ διαιρετὸς ὁ χρόνος.[107]

But if the 'now' is divided, there will be something of the past in the future and of the future if the past. For so far as it would be divided, this will separate past and future time. But the 'now' would not be at the same time and according to itself, but according to another. For the dividing is not according to [the 'now'] itself. But in addition to these things, part of the 'now' will be a past, part a future, and not always the same past or future. In fact, nor [will] the 'now' be the same. For time is divisible in many places.

Here Aristotle discusses a supposedly extended 'now,' which would have to exist for a 'now' to be a part of time. He points to the evident problems related to this understanding of the 'now.' If the 'now' would be extended, it would not just be a limit, but it would both stretch into the future and into the past relative to this limit, so that there would be a past in the future (on the 'future' side of the limit between past and future) and

---

[105] Aristotle, *Physica*, 239b8–9.
[106] Ibid., 234a11: ὥστε διαιρετὸν τὸ νῦν.
[107] Ibid., 234a11–19.

a future in the past (on the 'past' side of the limit between past and future), "But if the 'now' is divided, there will be something of the past in the future and of the future if the past. For so far as it would be divided, this will separate past and future time." This 'now' would be an unoriginal 'now,' since it would not be a limit but a continuum[108] in which the dividing line exists, "But the 'now' would not be at the same time and according to itself, but according to another." Aristotle notes in regard to the extended 'now' that "part of the 'now' will be a past, part a future, and not always the same past or future."[109] In fact, this supposed 'now' would have an "identity crisis," since there would be multiple points of division, "In fact, nor [will] the 'now' be the same."[110] Goldschmidt errs when he argues that the 'now' that serves as both the endpoint of the past and the starting point of the future rather are two different 'nows.'[111]

Coope finds Aristotle's arguments towards showing that the 'now' is merely *one* division, i.e. a single limit between the past and the future, "strangely unconvincing."[112] She objects against Aristotle's claims that, first, if the 'now' is extended it will be divisible and contain a past and a future, second, that any point within this continuum would be a division between a past and a future. She also points out that the one who believes in the existence of an extended 'now' would deny that there could be a division within this continuum.[113] Coope's objections are not difficult to refute from the viewpoint of Aristotle's understanding. First, an item with two limits (the beginning and the end of the extended 'now') would by definition constitute a divisible entity. Second, it goes without saying that regardless of where you make a division in this time continuum, what is before it would be past and what is after would be future relative to this division. Three, the assumption of the believer in an extended 'now' is not really an argument in itself. As for Coope's objections, we should also note

---

[108] As for the idea of a continuum consisting of indivisible components such as 'nows,' Aristotle (*Physics* 231b) rejects it since a continuum must consist of parts, "Moreover, if a succession of indivisibles could make up a continuum either of magnitude or time, that continuum could be resolved into its indivisible constituents. But, as we have seen, no continuum can be resolved into elements which have no parts." (Aristotle, *Physics*, 95).

[109] On this discussion, see Fred Miller (Miller. F.D., "Aristotle on the Reality of Time," *Archiv für die Geschichte der Philosophie* 56, (1974): 132–155, 131–34.

[110] For this discussion, cf. Torres, "La aporética del tiempo: Un análisis reconstructivo de Fis. Δ 10, 217b29–218b20", 220–21, 224–25.

[111] Goldschmidt, *Temps physique et temps tragique chez Aristote: Commentaire sur le Quatrième livre de la Physique (10–14) et sur la Poétique*, 154.

[112] Coope, *Time for Aristotle: Physics IV.10–14*, 22.

[113] Ibid., 22–23.

that they are of minor importance for our purposes here since we do not seek to argue against what Aristotle clearly claims on a certain point, but we rather seek to identify what the function and validity of the claims and arguments made in the ἀπορίαι are from the viewpoint of *Physics* IV.10–14 and the *Physics* as a whole.[114]

Aristotle thus rejects the concept of an extended 'now,' which means it cannot be *a* part of time, since it does not have any extension.[115]

6.7 In Context: The 'Now' as Different or Same

In the third, negative ἀπορία, the 'now' was portrayed as either a type with many tokens or a 'now' that forever expands or is infinitely extended. However, Aristotle explicitly rejects both these understandings of the 'now.' The idea of 'nows' as tokens of a type following one another must be rejected because extension-less entities cannot make up a series and because limits cannot be next to each other since they are limits of *some thing*. As for an extended 'now' it would like other finite items have to have more than one limit and it can therefore not go on forever. Also, Aristotle demonstrates what would happen if this were not the case—things happening today would be contemporaneous with ancient events. Jacques Dubois identifies the core of the problem:

> Tout le problème du temps paraît consister dans la difficulté d'accorder intelligiblement deux expériences primitives apparemment contradictoires: celle du flux de la durée et celle de l'actualité du présent.
>
> The whole problem of time seems to consist in the difficulty of intelligently reconciling two apparently contradictory basic experiences: that of the flow of duration and that of the currentness of the present.[116]

---

[114] In connection to the discussion of a possible extended 'now' we should note Aristotle's mention of another sense of τὸ νῦν in *Physics* IV.13, where from a cognitive-perceptive and pragmatic sense the 'now' refers to "not far off in time" as when referring to 'now' as earlier or later today (Aristotle, *Physics*, 411). Torres denotes the non-extended 'now' as the proper 'now' and the extended 'now' the improper one ("propia o impropiamente") (Torres, "La aporética del tiempo: Un análisis reconstructivo de Fis. Δ 10, 217b29–218b20", 223). This is going too far since both understandings of the 'now' have their legitimacy in their respective contexts (logical vs cognitive-perceptive, as argued above in Sect. 6.4).

[115] Cf. Sorabji, *Time, Creation and the Continuum: Theories in Antiquity and the Early Middle Ages*, 9.

[116] Dubois, *Le temps et l'instant selon Aristote (Physic. IV, 10–14)*, 142; my translation.

In several passages in his positive account, most explicitly so in *Physics* 219b9–15, it is evident that Aristotle indeed views the 'now' as both the 'same' and 'different.'[117] So different does his positive account seem compared to the discussion in the third ἀπορία that Hervé Barreau asks himself: "On peut se demander si Aristote s'est entièrement dégagé des apories sur l'instant qui ouvraient son étude sur le temps (218a6–218a 30) [One can ask oneself as to whether Aristotle has entirely freed himself from the aporias on the 'now' that introduce his study on time (218a6–218a30)]."[118] So, the question arises how he is able first to reject the sameness/differentness of the 'now/s' and then embrace it/them.

The answer to this question is found in the ambiguous use of 'same [τὸ αὐτό]' and 'different [ἕτερος].'[119] In the aporetic contrast as presented in the third ἀπορία, the concept of 'different' is used in terms of *identity*, i.e. not being the same entity, i.e. several 'nows' are following one another and therefore being 'different' from one another. As for the use of 'same' in the aporetic contrast, it is used both in the sense of *identity*, i.e. it is the one and same 'now,' and the 'same' in the sense of *an infinitely quantitative extension in time*; that is, the one and same identical 'now' remains the same while forever expanding/being infinitely extended throughout time. None of these understandings of 'different' and 'same'[120] find support in Aristotle's following chapters on time but are merely here presented as aporetic 'perplexing' elements that both must be rejected.

However, both 'different' and 'same' are polysemous and may be used in other senses to properly reflect Aristotle's actual position as to the 'now.' In regard to the concept of 'different' in relation to the 'now,' we should understand it in terms of a *quality*, i.e. a single 'now' that is different in terms of quality from one point to another,[121] but *not* in terms of identity

---

[117] Cf. Moreau (Joseph Moreau, "Le temps et l'instant selon Aristote (Phys. IV, 11, 219b9–220a1; 13, 222a10–29)," in *Naturphilosophie bei Aristoteles und Theophrast*, ed. Ingemar Düring, Verhandlungen (Heidelberg: Lothar Stiehm Verlag, 1969), 148).

[118] Barreau, "L'instant et le temps selon Aristote (Physique IV, 10–4, 217b29–224a17)", 216.

[119] The Greek for 'different [ἕτερος]' it is not used in the third ἀπορία, but is clearly implied in the context of understanding 'nows' as "one after another [ἄλλο καὶ ἄλλο]" and therefore 'different' from each other.

[120] Roark notes that there is evidence in *Physics* 262a28–b22 that Aristotle rejects the 'eternalist' 'now' (Roark, *Aristotle on Time: A Study of Physics*, 214).

[121] This differentness is analogous to the differentness of Koriscos in the Lyceum and the marketplace (Aristotle, *Physica*, 219b16–29).

in the sense of 'different ones' (i.e. multiple 'nows'). As for 'same,' we should understand it in the sense of identity, i.e. it is the one and same 'now,' but *not* the same in the sense of a quantity that remains the same and expands temporally without limit or is infinitely extended in time.

This updated understanding of 'different' and 'same' applied to the 'now' is what we find in Aristotle's positive account of time. The most illustrative passages in regard to this understanding of the 'now' are found in two passages close to one another in *Physics* 222a.

In *Physics* 222a, Aristotle states,

ἀλλὰ τοῦτ' οὐχ ὥσπερ ἐπὶ τῆς στιγμῆς μενούσης φανερόν. διαιρεῖ δὲ δυνάμει. καὶ ᾗ μὲν τοιοῦτο, αἰεὶ ἕτερον τὸ νῦν, ᾗ δὲ συνδεῖ, αἰεὶ τὸ αὐτό.[122]

But this ['now'] is not just as obvious as in the case of a fixed point. But it divides in potentiality [δυνάμει], and in so far as, on the one hand, it is such as this, the 'now' is always different, but, on the other, in so far as it unites, it is always the same.

Here Aristotle uses the analogy of a point,[123] just like in the third ἀπορία, as his point of departure when discussing the 'now.' The 'now,' on the one hand, divides time in potentiality, and in this sense it is always qualitatively different, "But it divides in potentiality [δυνάμει], and in so far as, on the one hand, it is such as this, the 'now' is always different." In potentiality the one 'now' thus *differs* in its role as divider. However, in its capacity of holding time together continuously, the one and same 'now' stays the same in actuality, "but, on the other, in so far as it unites, it is always the same." In other words, by the concept of potentiality/actuality both the moving 'now' that remains the same and the 'now' as different from one point to another must be accepted as part of Aristotle's concept of time. Wicksteed and Cornford's translation (or more properly, paraphrase) of this text is misleading when they translate "And in this potentiality one 'now' differs from another," for Aristotle is not talking about

---

[122] Ibid., 222a13–15.

[123] Aristotle (*Physics* 222a) expands on this analogy a few lines further down, explaining in which sense the point (just like the 'now') both differs from every other point as well as remaining the same throughout, "for if we are dividing the line, the point differs at every division, but if we regard the line as a single undivided one, the point that traces it is the same all along." (Aristotle, *Physics*, 409).

'different' in terms of identity (different 'nows'), but rather 'different' in the sense of the one and same 'now' that is qualitatively different from one point to another. This understanding is corroborated further down in *Physics* 222a,

> οὕτω καὶ τὸ νῦν τὸ μὲν τοῦ χρόνου διαίρεσις κατὰ δύναμιν, τὸ δὲ πέρας ἀμφοῖν καὶ ἑνότης· ἔστι δὲ ταὐτὸ καὶ κατὰ ταὐτὸ ἡ διαίρεσις καὶ ἡ ἕνωσις, τὸ δ' εἶναι οὐ ταὐτό.[124]

> In this way too the 'now,' on the one hand, is a divider of time according to potentiality [δύναμιν], but, on the other, the limit [πέρας] and uniter [ἑνότης] of both. But the divider [διαίρεσις] and the uniter [ἕνωσις] is the same and according to the same, but the 'being' [τὸ ... εἶναι] is not the same.

Here the 'now' is identified as a potential divider, "In this way too the 'now,' on the one hand, is a divider of time according to potentiality [δύναμιν]." At the same time the same 'now' is identified and described as "the limit [πέρας] and uniter [ἑνότης] of both."[125] That is, just as the 'now' serves as a potential divider it functions as an actual limit and uniter of "both," i.e. past and future time. In this capacity the 'now' travels through time[126] in its actuality and divides time in its potentiality and is therefore 'different' in one position relative to another along the temporal axis.[127] As Aristotle elaborates he further underlines that the 'now' in its capacity as divider and uniter is the very same 'now' from different perspectives, and these two functions pertain to this 'now,' "But the divider [διαίρεσις] and the uniter [ἕνωσις] is the same and according to the same."[128] That the 'now' is not the same in its accidental differentness, i.e.

---

[124] Aristotle, *Physica*, 222a17–20.

[125] This passage shows that Striowski errs when she argues that "The problem with understanding the now as always "other and other" (*heteron kai heteron*) is that it is not the now, but rather the *parts* of time that are another and another by virtue of the fact that they are not simultaneous" (Striowski, "Aristotle on Time and the Soul", 61).

[126] Mesch initially rejects the idea of "ein fliessendes Jetzt," but at the end of his discussion he seems to open up for such a possibility (Mesch, *Reflektierte Gegenwart: eine Studie über Zeit und Ewigkeit bei Platon, Aristoteles, Plotin und Augustinus*, 370, 385).

[127] Cf. McGinnis (McGinnis, "Making Time Aristotle's Way", 167).

[128] Tony Roark recognises that Aristotle understands that the 'now' as both the same and different, and argues that Aristotle's thinking echoes a text passage in Plato's *Parmenides* (Roark, *Aristotle on Time: A Study of Physics*, 213–214): Plato, *Parmenides*, ed. J. Burnet (1901), 156d1–e3; in this text, τὸ ἐξαίφνης 'the moment' may be understood as equivalent to the 'now.' Other texts passages that may be taken to be parallels to Aristotle's ἀπορία are *Parmenides* 217b33–218a3 and 218a3–8.

its 'being,' is expressed in the final clause, "but the 'being' [τὸ . . . εἶναι] is not the same."[129]

In her attempt to resolve the difficulty of the 'differentness' of the 'now,' Coope, on the basis of the concept of ceasing that is implied by "destroyed" in the third ἀπορία, asks the question "When has the now that was at five o'clock ceased to exist?" Her answer is: "It has first ceased to exist *in the time between five o'clock and the first actual now that is marked out after five o'clock.*"[130] Coope's question is wrongly put because the 'now' does not 'exist' (in an extended sense). Her solution assumes that the 'now' has extension in time. We discussed this in Sect. 6.6 and noted that Coope failed to demonstrate that the 'now' has extension. Therefore the 'now' does not exist in the sense of having extension, which means that since a 'now' does not begin to exist it cannot cease to exist. Commenting on Coope's example we could instead say that what ceases from the five o'clock 'now' and the next 'now' that we mark out is the time that lasts until the potential, second 'now.' Roark, discussing another passage on the same topic,[131] correctly comments that Aristotle's answer to the question "when does the now cease to be?" is "there is no such time."[132] Long before Roark, Simplicius drew the same conclusion, "For, if it has ceased to be, then since what ceases to be does so in time, it must cease to be at itself or at another 'now'. But it cannot cease to be at itself, for then it exists."[133] To Aristotle the 'now' is merely a limit, which means that Coope's solution would not be possible, or even relevant, from the viewpoint of Aristotle's thinking. However, more importantly, as already discussed above, is the fact that the sense in which 'different' is used about the 'now' in the third ἀπορία is not relevant from the viewpoint of Aristotle's positive account of time.

Richard Sorabji also understands the 'now' in the third ἀπορία as extended, "The sense of 'exist' here is 'be present,'" thus following the language of existence in the third ἀπορία that Aristotle uses about multiple

---

[129] Cf. Mesch's conclusion in regard to the sameness and differentness of the 'now' (Mesch, "Zeit", 467).

[130] Coope, *Time for Aristotle: Physics IV.10–14*, 28.

[131] *Physics* 262a28–b22 (Roark, *Aristotle on Time: A Study of Physics*, 214).

[132] Ibid., 215; Mesch makes the same general point (Mesch, *Reflektierte Gegenwart: eine Studie über Zeit und Ewigkeit bei Platon, Aristoteles, Plotin und Augustinus*, 370).

[133] Simplicius, *On Aristotle's Physics 4.1–5, 10–14*, 698 (p. 106).

'nows' following one another. He then offers a detailed argument as to the ceasing of a 'now' and its relation to the next 'now.'[134] Again, with the solution that we have presented above in regard to the polysemy of 'same [τὸ αὐτό]' and 'different [ἕτερος],' where the one and same 'now' is 'different' in different potential positions along the time continuum there is no 'ceasing "now" ' to be explained.

We conclude that Aristotle argues for an understanding of the 'now' as the one and same 'now' that moves through time, uniting continually and actually past and future, and this same 'now' as a potential divider in terms of differentness throughout time.

---

[134] Sorabji, *Time, Creation and the Continuum: Theories in Antiquity and the Early Middle Ages*, 10–12.

CHAPTER 7

Conclusion: From Aporia (ἀπορία) to Euporia (εὐπορία)

Abstract 'Aporia' refers either to a subjective mental state of perplexity or to the aporetic object of study. The *aporia* has the potential to bring the enquirer to a state of humility, making room for new thoughts to arise. The goal of the aporetic enquiry is to bring new insights and new knowledge by the reaching of an *euporia* 'a solution.' The existence of time is demonstrated to either be actual or potential. Time and the 'now' are perquisites for one another, where neither would exist without the other; time is located in the 'now' in combination with preceding and following time. Time is approached both from a mathematical-logic perspective as an extensionless limit between past and future time, and from a cognitive-perceptive point of view. Time is not a substance but takes part of substance by being modelled on the motion of a moving thing, a substance. The 'now' is not *a* part of time but still an important part in Aristotle's conceptualisation of time. The one and same 'now' is the *same* in actuality and accidentally *different* as a potential divider.

Keywords Aporia • Euporia • Actual existence of time • Potential existence of time • Cognition • Perception • Substance • 'Now' as partaker of substance • Motion • Moving thing • 'Now' as the same • 'Now' as different

At the outset of this enquiry it was noted that ἀπορία as a concept figures both as a subjective mental state of perplexity and a sense of being at a loss, and as an objective reality, the cause of this mental state, in terms of a concrete problem where two perspectives are pitted against one another, where one of these positions, in the best case scenario, has to be rejected, or in the worst, both. In the latter case the outcome is the falsification of two proposals, hopefully leading on to new formulations and a new ἀπορία where one of the options may be positively corroborated.

The ἀπορία is a tool used to bring the enquirer to a point of humility, to a position where all cards are put on the table, where all perspectives and points of view are reassessed and where the slate is wiped clean to make place for new thought to arise. The goal of the aporetic enquiry is to gain new insights, new knowledge. The aporetic moment is when the core of a problem or an aspect of a problem is formulated and brought out in the open in its naked, brute insurmountability to be faced in the struggle of a mind-mining exploration and to be the object of careful consideration.

The goal is the transition from ἀπορία to εὐπορία 'a solution,' where the *function* of the ἀπορία in various ways—depending on how it is constructed (whether explicitly or implicitly)—is to propel the thought process in a forward motion:

In Sects. 5.2 and 6.2 (The Existence or Non-existence of Time), the possible non-existence of time was contrasted against the unspoken *endoxa* that time indeed exists. Like Socrates demands a definition of virtue from Meno who has held speeches on the topic 'before large audiences on a thousand occasions' and still manages to derail his attempt,[1] so the readers are faced with the task of defending the fact of time's existence, an existence that anyone is aware of but only with much difficulty would be able to offer even shreds of evidence for. Nevertheless, the aporetic challenge inspires a quest for answers, where time is demonstrated to exist either actually or potentially.

In Sects. 5.3 and 6.3 (Time as Infinite Past and Future or Eternal 'Now'), the negative ἀπορία leaves the reader at a loss with two rejected proposals, i.e. time as located in the infinite past or future or in an eternally extended 'now.' However, the rejected leftovers are still helpful matter in the identification of a solution. The resolution of the ἀπορία is found in a

---

[1] Matthews, *Socratic Perplexity and the Nature of Philosophy*, 111.

7 CONCLUSION: FROM APORIA (ἀπορία) TO EUPORIA (εὐπορία) 79

synthesis of elements of the two dismissed proposals which thus serve as building materials towards the resolution. Time and the 'now' are perquisites for one another, where neither would exist without the other; time is located in the 'now' in combination with preceding and following time.

In Sects. 5.4 and 6.4 (*Time as a Cognitive-Perceptive or a Mathematical-Logical Category*), attention is brought to the aporetic contrast between mathematical-logical thought on time and a cognitive-perceptive approach, where there might be a temptation to overemphasise the former and treat the latter as pre-theoretical. The resolution is that Aristotle allows both perspectives to inform his thought on time, especially the latter when he argues that unperceived time—whether physically detected or cognitively imagined—might not even exist except in a very restricted sense. Strictly speaking then the cognitive-perceptive approach wins the day since time in the fullest sense does not exist without the detection of a conscious mind.

In Sects. 5.5 and 6.5 (Time as Partaker of Substance or not), the question of time's partaking in substance or not is brought to the fore with a mostly negative (but tentative) tendency in focus. The weak expectation as to the possibility of time partaking in substance turns into a full reversal in the corroboration of time's partaking in substance. The aporetic portrayal of time as a categorial lone wolf, apparently cut off from a place in Aristotle's theology (metaphysics), is cancelled with the realisation that time is the last outpost in the triad *magnitude > motion > time* and ultimately in symbiotic interdependence with motion and the underlying moving thing, a substance; in this manner time is a partaker of substance.

In Sects. 5.6 and 6.6 ('Nows' as the Parts of Time or not), the discussion on the 'now' as a part of time hinges on the semantics of 'part,' whether as an element of a substance (and therefore having extension) or as a part in Aristotle's metaphysics of time; in Aristotle's syntax of time the 'now' most assuredly makes a comeback from first having been denied parthood, figuring centre-stage as the guarantor of and point of departure for the parts of time, the past and the future. The initial threat of denying the 'now' parthood provokes a reconceptualisation and recontextualisation at the level of temporal metaphysics, where its central place is a given; although not *a* part, the 'now' is still a central part in Aristotle's conceptualisation of time.

Finally, Sects. 5.7 and 6.7 (The 'Now' as Different or Same) deal with the only typically and explicitly constructed ἀπορία, which is very evidently constructed to depend on the polysemy of τὸ αὐτό 'the same' and ἕτερος 'different.' In the first set of senses of the pair, as portrayed in the ἀπορία, 'different' and 'the same' are both rejected. However, what seems to be a complete failure inspires the usage of a second set of senses of 'the same' and 'different' that allows a synthesis of the two in terms of features attributed to the one and same 'now' in potentiality and actuality in Aristotle's temporal economy, so that the 'now' remains the same in actuality in its capacity as the constantly moving borderline between the past and the future, while at the same time accidentally different at each new point of division as a potential divider.

Bibliography

Aguirre, Javier. *Dialéctica y filosofía primera. Lectura de la Metafísica de Aristóteles.* Zaragoza: Prensas de la Universidad de Zaragoza, 2015

Annas, Julia. "Aristotle, Number and Time." *The Philosophical Quarterly (1950-)* 25, no. 99 (1975): 97–113

Aristotle. *Analytica priora et posteriora.* ed. W.D. Ross.

———. *De interpretatione.* ed. L. Minio-Paluello.

———. *Aristotelis Physica.* ed. W. D. Ross. Oxford: Clarendon Press, 1950 (repr. 1966 (1st edn. corr.)

———. *Aristotle: The Nicomachean Ethics; a commentary by H. H. Joachim.* ed. D. A. Rees. Oxford: Clarendon, 1951

———. *Topica.* ed. W. D. Ross. 1960

———. *Aristotle. Topics. Books I and VIII. Translated with Commentary by Robin Smith.* Oxford: Oxford University Press, 1997

———. *Metaphysica.* ed. W.D. Ross.

———. *Physica.* ed. W.D. Ross.

———. *Physics.* Translated by Philip H. Wicksteed & Francis M. Cornford. ed. Jeffrey Henderson. 1929

———. *Topica.* Translated by E. S. Forster. ed. E. S. Forster. 1960

———. *De anima.* ed. W.D. Ross. 1961

———. *Analytica priora et posteriora.* ed. W.D. Ross.: 1964

Aubenque, Pierre. "Sens et fonction de l'aporie socratique." *Philosophie antique. Problèmes, Renaissances, Usages* no. 3 (2003): 2–20

———. "Sur la notion aristotélicienne d'aporie." In *Aristote et les problèmes de méthode: Communications présentées au Symposium Aristotelicum tenu à*

Louvain du 24 août au 1 Septembre 1960, ed. Suzanne Mansion, Paris: Publications Universitaires de Louvain, 1980

Barnes, Jonathan. "Aristotle and the Methods of Ethics." *Revue internationale de philosophie* 34; 133/134, (1980): 490–511

Barreau, Hervé. "L'instant et le temps selon Aristote (Physique IV, 10–14, 217b29–224a17)." *Revue philosophique de Louvain* 66, (1968): 213–238

———. "Le traité aristotélicien du temps." *Revue Philosophique de la France et de l'Étranger* 163, (1973): 401–437

Berti, Enrico. "Aristote et la méthode dialectique du Parmenide de Platon." *Revue internationale de philosophie* 34; 133/134, (1980): 341–358

Böhme, Gernot. *Zeit und Zahl. Studien zur Zeittheorie bei Platon, Aristoteles, Leibnitz und Kant*. Frankfurt a. M.: V. Klostermann, 1974

Bolotin, David. "Aristotle's Discussion of Time: An Overview." *Ancient Philosophy* 17, (1997): 47–62

Bostock, David. "Aristotle's Account of Time." *Phronesis* 25, no. 2 (1980): 148–169

Boudreault, Pierre-Luc. "Aristotle's Account of Time: A Moderate Realism." The University of Western Ontario, 2020

Brisard, Frank. "A Critique of Localism in and About Tense Theory." Ph.D. thesis, University of Antwerp, 1999

Bruder, Michael. "The Time of Our Lives: Aristotle on Time, Temporal Perception, Recollection, and Habituation." McMaster University, 2011

Buddensiek, Friedemann. "Aporia in Aristotle's Metaphysics B." In *The Aporetic Tradition in Ancient Philosophy*, ed. George Karamanolis, and Vasilis Politis, 137–154. Cambridge: Cambridge University Press, 2018

Castelli, Laura M. *Aristotele. Fisica. Libro IV*. Roma: Carocci editore, 2012

Cavagnaro-Stuijt, Elena. *Aristotele e il tempo: analisi di Physica, 4.10–14*. Bologna: Il mulino, 1995

Closs Traugott, Elizabeth. "Spatial Expressions of Tense and Temporal Sequencing." *Semiotica* 15, no. 3 (1975): 207–230

Collobert, Catherine. *Traité du temps: Physique, livre IV, 10–14*. Paris: Èdition Kimé, 2004

Coope, Ursula. *Time for Aristotle: Physics IV.10–14*. Oxford: Clarendon Press, 2005

Dubois, Jacques Marcel. *Le temps et l'instant selon Aristote (Physic. IV, 10–14)*. Paris: Desclée de Brouwer, 1967

Dunshirn, Alfred. "Das ‚Jetzt' in Aristoteles' Zeittheorie: Zu Physik IV 11, 219 b 10–25." *Wiener Studien* Band 119/2006, (2006): 63–75

Düring, Ingemar. *Aristotle in the Ancient Biographical Tradition*. Vol. LXIII. Göteborgs Universitets Årsskrift, Stockholm: Almqvist & Wiksell, 1957

Erler, Michael. "Aporia." *Brill's New Pauly* https://doi.org/10.1163/1574-9347_bnp_e128880 (accessed 28 October, 2017).

Evans, Vyvyan. *The Structure of Time: Language, Meaning and Temporal Cognition*. Amsterdam/Philadelphia: John Benjamins Publishing Company, 2003

Evans, Vyvyan, and Melanie Green. *Cognitive Linguistics: An Introduction.* Edinburgh: Edinburgh University Press, 2006

Falcon, Andrea. "Aristotle on Time and Change." ed. Hether Dyke, and Adrian Bardon, 47–58. Oxford: Wiley Blackwell, 2013

Flaherty, Michael G. *A Watched Pot: How We Experience Time.* New York: New York University Press, 1999

Fleischman, Suzanne. "The Past and the Future." *Berkeley Linguistics Society* 8, (1983): 322–334

Geeraerts, Dirk. "Cognitive Semantics." In *The Routledge Handbook of Cognitive Linguistics*, ed. Xu Wen, and John R. Taylor, 19–29. New York: Routledge, 2021

Karamanolis, George, and Vasilis Politis. "Introduction." In *The Aporetic Tradition in Ancient Philosophy*, ed. George Karamanolis, and Vasilis Politis, 1–8. Cambridge: Cambridge University Press, 2018

Ghins, Michel. "Two Difficulties with Regard to Aristotle's Treatment of Time." *Revue de Philosophie Ancienne* 9, no. 1 (1991): 83–98

Givón, Talmy. *On Understanding Grammar.* New York: Academic, 1979

Goddard, Cliff. "Natural Semantic Metalanguage." In *The Routledge Handbook of Cognitive Linguistics*, ed. Xu Wen, and John R. Taylor, 93–110. New York: Routledge, 2021

Goldschmidt, Victor. *Temps physique et temps tragique chez Aristote: Commentaire sur le Quatrième livre de la Physique (10–14) et sur la Poétique.* Paris: Librarie Philosophique J. Vrin, 1982

Grant, Edward. *A History of Natural Philosophy: From the Ancient World to the Nineteenth Century.* Cambridge: Cambridge University Press, 2007

Harry, Chelsea C. *Chronos in Aristotle's Physics: On the Nature of Time.* London: Springer, 2015

Hussey, Edward. *Aristotle's Physics: Books III and IV, translated with notes by Edward Hussey.* Oxford: Clarendon Press, 1983

Ilting, Karl-Heinz. "Aporie." In *Handbuch philosophischer Grundbegriffe*, München: Kösel-Verlag, 1973

Inwood, Michael. "Aristotle on the Reality of Time." In *Aristotle's Physics: A Collection of Essays*, ed. Lindsay Judson, 151–178. Oxford: Oxford University Press, 1991

Kretzmann, Norman. "Time Exists-but Hardly, or Obscurely." *Proceedings of the Aristotelian Society, Supplementary Volumes (Published by Wiley-Blackwell on behalf of the Aristotelian Society)*, 50, (1976): 91–114

Langacker, Ronald W. "Cognitive Grammar." *The Oxford Handbook of Linguistic Analysis* (2015): 99–120. https://doi.org/10.1093/oxfordhb/9780199677 078.013.0005

Lugarini, Leo. *Aristotele e l'idea della filosofia.* 2 riveduta ed. Firenze: La Nuova Italia, 1972

Matthews, Gareth B. *Socratic Perplexity and the Nature of Philosophy.* Oxford: Oxford University Press, 1999

McGinnis, Jon. "Making Time Aristotle's Way." *Apeiron* 36, no. 2 (2003): 143–170

———. "A Review of Tony Roark: Aristotle on Time: A Study of Physics." *Philosophical Review* XXXII, no. 6 (2012): 518–520

Mesaroş, Claudiu. "Aristotle on Becoming and Meanings of Time." In *The Time is Now. Essays on the Philosophy of Becoming*, ed. Mihaela Gligor, Bucharest: Zeta Books, 2020

Mesch, Walter. *Reflektierte Gegenwart: eine Studie über Zeit und Ewigkeit bei Platon, Aristoteles, Plotin und Augustinus.* Frankfurt am Main: Klostermann, 2003

———. "Zeit." In *Aristoteles Handbuch: Leben - Werk - Wirkung*, ed. Christof Rapp, and Klaus Corcilius, Berlin: J.B. Metzler Verlag, 2021

Miller, F. D. "Aristotle on the Reality of Time." *Archiv für die Geschichte der Philosophie* 56, (1974): 132–155

Moreau, Joseph. "Le temps et l'instant selon Aristote (Phys. IV, 11, 219b9–220a1; 13, 222a10–29)." In *Naturphilosophie bei Aristoteles und Theophrast*, ed. Ingemar Düring, 147–153. Heidelberg: Lothar Stiehm Verlag, 1969

Nylund, Jan H. "The Prague School of Linguistics and its Influence on New Testament Language Studies." In *The Language of the New Testament. Context, History, and Development*, ed. Stanley E. Porter, and Andrew W. Pitts, Leiden/Boston: Brill, 2013

Nylund, Jan H. "The Potential of Linguistic Theories in the Study of Aspect and Tense in Ancient Greek, With Particular Attention to New Testament Greek." (Ph.D. thesis, Lund University, 2024)

Oakley, Todd. "Image Schemas." In *The Oxford Handbook of Cognitive Linguistics*, ed. Dirk Geeraerts, and Hubert Cuyckens, 214–235. Oxford: Oxford University Press, 2007

Owen, G. E. L. "Aristotle on Time." In *Motion and Time, Space and Matter: Interrelations in the History of Philosophy and Science*, ed. Peter Machamer, and Robert Turnbull, 3–27. Columbus: Ohio State University Press, 1976

Philoponus, Johannes. *Philoponus: On Aristotle Physics 4.10–14.* Translated by Sarah Broadie. Ancient Commentators on Aristotle, London: Bloomsbury Publishing, 2011

Plato. *Timaeus* (Bury).

———. *Parmenides.* ed. J. Burnet. 1901

———. *Meno.* ed. J. Burnet. 1903a

———. *Protagoras.* ed. J. Burnet. 1903b

Politis, Vasilis. "Aristotle on Aporia and Searching in Metaphysics." In *Proceedings of the Boston Area Colloquium in Ancient Philosophy* 18(1), 145–182. 2003

———. *The Structure of Enquiry in Plato's Early Dialogues.* Cambridge: Cambridge University Press, 2015

Rapp, Christof. "Aporia and Dialectical Method in Aristotle." In *The Aporetic Tradition in Ancient Philosophy*, ed. George Karamanolis, and Vasilis Politis, 112–136. Cambridge: Cambridge University Press, 2018

Roark, Tony. *Aristotle on Time: A Study of Physics*. Cambridge: Cambridge University Press, 2011

Rossitto, Cristina. "La dialettica e il suo ruolo nella metafisica di Aristotele." *Rivista di Filosofia neo-scolastica* 85; /2/4, (1993): 370–424

———. *Studi sulla dialettica in Aristotele*. Napoli: Bibliopolis, 2000

Ruggiu, Luigi. *Aristotele: Fisica; saggio introduttivo, traduzione, note e apparati*. Milano: Rusconi Libri, 1995

Seissl, Thomas. "Aristotle's "Now" and the Definition of Time: Method and Exegesis in Simplicius' Interpretation of Physics IV. 10." *History of Philosophy & Logical Analysis* 26, (2023): 366–386

Simplicius. *On Aristotle's Physics 4.1–5, 10–14*. Translated by James O. Urmson. The Ancient Commentators on Aristotle, London: Duckworth, 1992

Sorabji, Richard. *Time, Creation and the Continuum: Theories in Antiquity and the Early Middle Ages*. London: Duckworth, 1983

Stein, Nathanael. "Aristotle on Parts of Time and Being in Time." *The Review of Metaphysics* 69, no. 3 (2016): 495–518

Striowski, Andra. "Aristotle on Time and the Soul." Ph.D. thesis, University of Ottawa, 2016

Talmy, Leonard. *Toward a Cognitive Semantics, 2 Volumes*. Cambridge, Mass.: MIT press, 2000

Tay, Dennis. "Image Schemas." In *The Routledge Handbook of Cognitive Linguistics*, ed. Xu Wen, and John R. Taylor, 161–172. New York: Routledge, 2021

Themistius. *Themistius: On Aristotle Physics 4*. Translated by Robert B. Todd. Ancient Commentators on Aristotle, London: Bloomsbury Publishing, 2003

Torres, Jorge. "La aporética del tiempo: Un análisis reconstructivo de Fis. Δ 10, 217b29–218b20." *Ordia Prima* 8/9, (2009/2010): 211–234

Turner, Mark. "Opening Commentary: Polytropos and Communication in the Wild." In *The Cambridge Handbook of Cognitive Linguistics*, ed. Barbara Dancygier, 93–98. Cambridge: Cambridge University Press, 2017

Ungerer, Friedrich, and Hans-Jörg Schmid. *An Introduction to Cognitive Linguistics*. Harlow: Longman, 1996

van Emde Boas, Evert, Albert Rijksbaron, Luuk Huitink, and Mathieu de Bakker. *The Cambridge Grammar of Classical Greek*. Cambridge: Cambridge University Press, 2019

Waterlow, Sarah. "Aristotle's Now." *The Philosophical Quarterly (1950-)* 34, no. 135 (1984): 104–128

Wen, Xu, and Canzhong Jiang. "Embodiment." In *The Routledge Handbook of Cognitive Linguistics*, ed. Xu Wen, and John R. Taylor, 145–160. New York: Routledge, 2021

General Index[1]

A
Absolute 'now,' The, 52, 53
Actual, 67
Actual existence, 52
Actualisation, 50
Actuality, 49, 50, 66, 67, 73, 74
Adhesion, 37
After, The, 30, 31, 33, 42, 43, 61
Aguirre, Javier, 18n36
Alexander of Aphrodisias, 7n16
Annas, Julia, 67n95
Apollodorus, 7n16
Aporetic, 2–4, 15, 16, 19n42, 21, 24, 37
   contrast, 2, 4, 38, 40–43, 47, 55, 72, 79
   material, 3
   passages, 25
   statements, 7
   text, 8
Aporia, viii
   as dialectically structured textual tool, 2
   as a mental state of perplexity, 15, 15n10
   as perplexity, 15, 47
   as subjective mental state of perplexity, 78
Aporiai, vii, viii
   See also Ἀπορία
Aristotle's metaphysics, vii–viii, 3, 64
Aristotle's negative account of time, 2, 25, 36
Aristotle's research methodology, 24
Aristotle's temporal economy, 80
Aristotle's theology, 79
Aristotle's use of the term ἀπορία, 15
Aristotle's positive account of time, 2, 3, 7, 10, 72, 73, 75
Aubenque, Pierre, 15, 16, 47
Augustine, 7n16
Awareness of the passage time, 59
Awareness of time, 60

---

[1] Note: Page numbers followed by 'n' refer to notes.

B

Barnes, Jonathan, 39n4
Barreau, Hervé, 8, 33n36, 72
Before, The, 30, 33, 42, 43, 61
Being, The, 30, 33, 42, 49, 64, 65, 74, 75
Benchmark for the measurement of time, The, 68
Berti, Enrico, 18n34
Bodily experience, 51
Böhme, Gernot, 63
Bolotin, David, 6, 7n18
Bostock, David, 65n83, 68n102
Boudreault, Pierre-Luc, 6
Bounded space, 65
Brisard, Frank, 66n87
Bruder, Michael, 6, 61
Buddensiek, Friedemann, 17
Böhme, Gernot, 63

C

Castelli, Laura, 26n14, 28n17
Cause of perplexity [ἀπορία], The, 15
Cavagnaro-Stuijt, Elena, 6, 8, 26n14, 27n15
Chrysippus, 7n16
Circular motion, 68n103
Closs Traugott, Elizabeth, 66n87
Cognitive, 50, 62
    conceptualisation, 60
    dissonance, 47
    linguistics, viii, 3, 51
    perception of the now, The, 33
    representation, 51
    science, viii, 3, 51, 61–62
Cognitive-perceptual, 59, 79
Cognitive-perceptual language, viii, 3, 61
Cognitive-subjective reflection, 41
Cohesion, 37
Collective embodied mind, 51

Collobert, Catherine, 26n11, 26n14
Conceived time, 51
Conceptual projection, 65
Conflicting viewpoints, 2
Conscious mind, The, 79
Constant perception of time, The, 41
Container, 65
Continuity, 64, 65
Continuum, 70, 70n108
Coope, Ursula, 6, 9, 25n9, 26n13, 26n14, 27n15, 28n17, 48, 53, 54, 70, 75
Cornford, Francis M., 73
Correlation between time and conscience, The, 61
Cosmic motion, 67, 68n102
Cosmic time, 26n11, 51, 67
Cosmological dimension of time, The, 51

D

De caelo, 51n21
Dialectic, 16
Dialectical challenge, 10
Differentness of the now, The, 75n129
Difficulties, 17–21, 24, 47
Diodorus Cronus, 7n16
Division, 64, 65
Dubois, Jacques, 71
Düring, Ingemar, 24n3

E

Elusive now, The, 31
Empirical approach, 59
Empirical observations, 62
Endoxa, 38, 39, 78
Erler, Michael, 14n8
Eternalist 'now,' The, 72n120
Eternal now, The, 40, 55

Εὐπορία 'solution, 4, 14, 19, 20, 47, 78
Euporia, viii
Evans, Vyvyan, 61
Existence of time, The, 39, 54, 55n40, 56, 57, 62, 78
Experienced 'now,' The, 57, 58
Extended now, The, 69–71, 75
Extension-less present 'now,' The, 55

F
Factual statements, 8
Falcon, Andrea, 2n2
Figure-ground segregation, 51
Fleischman, Suzanne, 66n87
Flaherty, Michael, 61
Future time, 27, 28, 29n21, 30, 31, 39, 40, 42, 50, 52, 69, 74, 76

G
Gaining of new knowledge, The, 7
Gestalt psychology, 51
Gestalt whole, 51
Ghins, Michel, 67
Global aporetic contrasts, 37
Goal, 19, 21
Goldschmidt, Victor, 54, 56, 57, 70
Governing statements, 3
Green, Melanie, 61

H
Harry, Chelsea, 6, 9n32, 25n10, 27n15, 51n21, 56, 66n88
Heroes in Sardinia, The, 59
Holistic sensory-perceptual experiences, 65
Hussey, Edward, 26n11, 26n14, 27n15, 28n17
Hylomorphic, 52

I
Illimitability, 65n84
Iltinger, Karl-Heinz, 17n31
Image schemas, 65, 65n86
Impression through the body, 60
Inclusio, 25
Infinitely quantitative extension in time, 72
Infinite time, 27, 56
Insurmountable problem, 17, 20
Interdependence between time and the now, The, 57
Interpretive keys, 3
Introspective experience, 62
Inwood, Michael, 6, 55n40, 66–68

J
Joachim, Harold H., 57
Johannes Philoponus, 7, 9, 39n7

K
Karamanolis, George, 15
Knowledge, 2, 16, 18–20, 78
Koriscos, 72n121
Kretzmann, Norman, 6, 8, 39, 57n49

L
Limit, 32, 50, 55, 56, 69–71
Limithood, 33
Local aporetic contrasts, 37
Locomotion, 65
Lyceum, 72n121
Lycophron, 49

M
Magnitude, 64, 65, 65n84, 69, 70n108, 79
Magnitude > motion > time, 65

Mathematics, 58
Matthews, Gareth, 15, 19n42
McGinnis, Jon, 6, 9, 16, 26n14
Meno, 14n8, 17, 78
Mental state of ἀπορία, The, 15, 20, 47
Mesaroş, Claudiu, 68n103
Mesch, Walter, 6, 8, 9, 26n14, 29n20, 37n1, 63, 74n126, 75n129, 75n132
Metaphysical enquiries, 21
Methodological approaches for the study of nature, 58
Methodological aspect of ἀπορία, The, 14n8
Miller, Fred, 70n109
Mind, The, 41, 59, 60
Mon-moving objects, 68
Moreau, Joseph, 72n117
Motion, 54, 56, 57, 64–68, 65n84, 66n88, 79
Motion of celestial bodies, The, 67, 68
Motion of the sphere, The, 68
Motion of the universe, The, 51
Movement in the mind, 60
Moving 'now,' The, 73
Moving object, The, 67
Moving thing, The, 57, 67, 68

N

Natural science, 10
Natural Semantic Metalanguage, 62
Nature of time, The, 2n2
Negative ἀπορία, The, 17, 36, 71, 78
Negative inclusio, 3
Neuroscience, 51, 60
Nicomachean Ethics VII, 17
Nonbeings, 52
Non-existence, 52
Non-existence of time, The, 10, 38, 39

Non-existing time, 52
Non-present existence, 52
Now, The, 28–32, 29n21, 39, 42, 43, 50, 52–57, 60, 67–76, 70n108, 74n128, 79, 80
  as the actual limit and uniter of time, 74
  as the basis for time's continuity, 57
  as 'different' in quality, 72
  as 'different,' 72, 75
  as a divider of time, 33, 73, 74
  as foregrounded, 52
  as the identical entity, 31, 43
  as the limit of time, 74, 75
  as a mathematical abstract limit, 57
  as mediator, 55
  as potential divider of time, 74
  as a psychological entity, 58
  as the 'same,' 72
  as a type with many tokens, 31, 42, 43
  as the uniter of time, 74

O

Oakley, Todd, 65
Object *qua* moving, The, 67, 68
Objective sense of aporia, The, 2, 14
Off-line processing, 60
Olympic Games, 49, 50
On-line perceptual experience, 60
Ontologial dependence of motion on substance, The, 65n83
Ontological dependence of time on motion, The, 65n83
Owen, G. E. L., 54

P

Parthood, 39, 42, 79
Parthood of the now, The, 43

Past time, 27, 28, 29n21, 30, 39, 40, 42, 50, 52, 69, 74, 76, 79
Path, 65
Perceive, 33
Perceiving mind, The, 33, 61
Perception as methodology, 59
Perception of the mind, The, 53
Perception of time, The, 27, 40, 41, 58
Perceptual experience, 65
Perplexing, 2
Perplexity, 19, 20
Phainomena, 10, 48
Philoponus, Johannes, 9, 30n30
Place, 63
Plato, vii, 3, 7, 14, 15, 15n10, 15n12, 20, 51, 74n128
Plato's dialogues, 20
Platonic mental state of ἀπορία, The, 15
Platonic sense of ἀπορία, The, 15
Point, 32, 54, 73
Politis, Vasilis, 15, 15n10, 18, 19n42, 20
Polysemy, 72, 76, 79
Poseidonius, 7n16
Positive account of time, vii
Positive ἀπορία, The, 18, 36, 40, 42
Potential, 67
Potential existence, 52
Potentiality, 49, 50, 66, 67, 73, 74
Pre-conceptual experience, 65
Pretheoretical understanding of time, 10
Psychology, 51
Puzzlement, 19
Puzzles, The, 2n2, 10, 11

Q
Quality, 63, 64
Quantity, 63–65

R
Rapp, Christof, 16
Rational approach, 59
Rational thought, 62
Reason as methodology, 59
Roark, Tony, 6, 10, 11, 11n38, 48, 48n5, 49, 56n43, 67n94, 72n120, 74n128, 75
Rossitto, Cristina, 15n13
Rotation of the sun and the moon, The, 68
Ruggiu, Luigi, 26n14, 58, 63

S
Sameness of the 'now,' The, 72, 75n129
Seissl, Thomas, 7n16, 50n13, 56n46
Self, The, 51
Sensory experience, 62
Sequential scanning, 51
Shared neuroanatomical and cognitive architecture, 62
Simplicius, 7, 8, 27n15, 30n30, 50n13, 75
Socrates, 14n8, 17, 78
Solution, 2, 18, 20, 47
Sophistical endoxa, 11
Sorabji, Richard, 6, 7n16, 10, 26n14, 27n15, 38n2, 50n14, 75
State of mind of being perplexed, 14
Stein, Nathanael, 6, 10, 11n39, 48, 51n21, 52
Striowski, Andra, 6, 8, 26n11, 26n13, 26n14, 27n15, 50, 74n125
Subjective-cognitive viewpoints, 27
Subjective consciousness, 57
Subjective sense of aporia, The, 2
Subjective state of perplexity, The, 47
Subjective state of ἀπορία, The, 14, 47
Substance, 26, 26n14, 27, 39, 41, 42, 62–64, 68, 79
Summary scanning, 51

Sun, The, 68
Symbiotic relationship between the 'now' and time, The, 56

T
Talmy, Leonard, 66n87
Tay, Dennis, 65n86
Temporal metaphysics, 79
Themistius, 7, 8, 39n5
Third ἀπορία, The, 72, 73, 75
Time as a cognitive entity, 53
Time as a measurer of motion, 66
Time as a number, 66
Time as partaker of substance, 79
Time continuum, 70
Time from a macro-perspective, 67
Torres, Jorge, 6, 9, 26n11, 26n14, 27n15, 29n21, 70n110, 71n114
Triple ἀπορία, The, 2, 15, 24, 68
Turner, Mark, 60

U
Underlying constantly moving substance of time, The, 68
Underlying moving thing, The, 79
Underlying thing, The, 63, 64, 67, 68
Unperceived time, 79

V
Visual Scanning, 51

W
Waterlow, Sarah, 56n46
Whole and the part, The, 59
Wicksteed, Philip H., 73

Z
Zero point, 2, 39

Index Locorum[1]

A
Analytica priora et posteriora
  75a22–23, 14n1
  82a18–19, 14n2
  89b32–34, 24n4
  90b1–2, 14n3
  98a35–36, 14n3

M
Metaphysics, viii, 3, 79
  B, 18
  III.1, 15, 47
  995a24–995b2, 18
  995b2–4, 19n42

O
On the Heavens (De caelo), 51n21
On Interpretation
  16a5–8, 62n73
On the Soul
  402b14–16, 14n3
  408a34–b1, 14n3

P
Parmenides, 74n128
  156d1–e3, 74n128
  217b33–218a3, 74n128
  218a3–8, 74n128
Physics, 58
  IV.10, vii, viii, 2, 3, 6–8, 11, 25
  IV.10–14, vii, 2, 6, 56, 71
  IV.11–14, 3, 4, 9, 10
  IV.13, 50, 53, 71n114
  IV.14, 51, 67
  VIII, 51n21
  185b, 49
  189a, 58
  189a4–8, 58n55
  190a, 63
  190a32–190b1, 63n80
  202b, 58n54

[1] Note: Page numbers followed by 'n' refer to notes.

206a, 49
206a21–25, 49n8
206a22-25, 27n15
206a23, 27
217b30–33, 24n1
217b32–33, 38n3
217b33–218a3, 25–28
217b33–218a30, 36, 38
218a3–218a8, 28n16
218a6-218a30, 72
218a8–218a30, 30n27
218a31–33, 25n6
218b, 59
218b21–23, 59n58
218b–219b, 61
218b26, 60n60
218b29–32, 60n61
219a, 60
219a30–31, 61n69
219a31–b1, 61n70
219a4–8, 60n63
219a–b, 61
219b16–29, 72n121
219b–220a, 56
219b33–220a2, 57n48
219b9–15, 72
220a4–5, 57n48
220b, 64
222a, 73, 73n123, 74
222a13–15, 73n122
222a17–20, 74n124
222a20–22, 50n15
223a, 61, 66, 67
223a16–17, 61n72
223a18–21, 66n89
223a25–28, 61
223b21–224a2, 67n100
223b21–23, 68n101
231b, 70n108
234a, 69
234a11, 69n106
234a24–25, 53n33
234a24–3, 53
234a31, 54n36
237a, 53
237a10–11, 54n38
237a11–15, 53n29
239b, 68
239b8–9, 69n105
241a, 54
241a2–6, 54n37
251b, 54, 55, 66, 67
251b19–20, 55n40
251b19–26, 55n41
251b26–27, 66n91
262a28–b22, 72n120, 75n131
Posterior Analytics
  II.1, 24
Protagoras
  324d-e, 15n12

T
Timaeus, vii, 3, 51
  37c6-d7, 51n20
Topics, 16, 18
  I.2, 16, 17, 47
  IV.6, 15